D0629328

Cost

OF

Living

Cost

OF

Living

ESSAYS

Emily Maloney

 HENRY HOLT AND COMPANY   NEW YORK

Henry Holt and Company
Publishers since 1866
120 Broadway
New York, New York 10271
www.henryholt.com

Henry Holt® and Ⓗ® are registered trademarks of Macmillan Publishing Group, LLC.

These essays first appeared in different form in the following publications: "I Stalked My Psychiatrist" in the *Atlantic*, and "Cost of Living" and "Something for the Pain" in the *Virginia Quarterly Review*. "Cost of Living" was also reprinted in *Best American Essays 2017*.

Library of Congress Cataloging-in-Publication Data is available

ISBN: 9781250213297

Our books may be purchased in bulk for promotional, educational, or business use. Please contact your local bookseller or the Macmillan Corporate and Premium Sales Department at (800) 221-7945, extension 5442, or by e-mail at MacmillanSpecialMarkets@macmillan.com.

First Edition 2022

Designed by Meryl Sussman Levavi

Printed in the United States of America

1   3   5   7   9   10   8   6   4   2

For Ori, my light

In New York's Garment District, a little old man was hit by a car. While waiting for an ambulance, the policeman tucked a blanket under the guy's chin and asked, "Are you comfortable?"

The man said, "I make a nice living."

—Henny Youngman

Contents

This is a true story, though names and details have been changed.

A Note on This Book

I don't remember 2005, but I have the medical records.

When I set out to write this book, I imagined neat little blocks of prose, perfectly arranged. I could simply tell you what happened. How I survived. What I did. I thought of this book as a guide for people who had it happen to them. That everyone seems to have medical debt, or know someone who does. And that there would be a clean, orderly way to resolve the issues that came up. I was misdiagnosed, I would explain. It's so easy now.

The truth is, I kept talking to women whose experiences mirrored mine. Who had been diagnosed with some injury or illness, and that illness tended not to be a medical failure but a failure of personality. Feelings were our fault, and we felt them too much. I wanted so badly to be slotted into some easy category, some boxes to check, some medication to take. We had entered the biological revolution in psychiatry, my doctor had explained, and could take medication the way diabetics counted insulin. That there was a one-to-one relationship between medical diagnosis and medication administration. But this wasn't true.

I had believed that doctors knew everything. That I could fix myself, my life, with the right doctor or the right medication or more money. That the medical world, that science itself, was black and white. Yes or no. Hypothesis proven or disproven. I had always put my trust in science; I believed that the dollar answered to the doctor.

I thought: If I could just do this work, maybe I could pay my debt.

Cost of Living

In 2008, the hospital where I worked—a Level II trauma center just outside Chicago—was $54 million in debt. Everyone seemed to be aware of this fact; the figure floated beneath the surface of all our conversations, an unspoken rigidity we seemed to bump up against everywhere we turned. We were to be careful when we distributed small stuffed animals to unhappy children in the ER, were told to dispense fewer scrub tops to adolescents with dislocated shoulders and bloodied shirts, to pay attention to the way that canes seemed to walk off as if under their own power. Everything cost money, Helene, our nursing manager, reminded us, even if the kid was screaming and had to get staples in his scalp. I was an ER tech then, someone who drew blood, performed EKGs, and set up suture trays. Most of my knowledge of the world of the ER came through direct patient care. If a nurse or a doctor needed something for a patient, I'd get it for them. I'd run into the stockroom, sort through yards of plastic tubing, through dozens of disposable plastic pieces, acres of gauze. We—the techs—were expected to guard against the depletion of resources. Helene seemed to remind us at every available opportunity by tacking notes up on the bulletin board in the staff break room. PLEASE CONSERVE YOUR RESOURCES. ONLY USE WHAT IS NECESSARY. These notes were pinned next to our Press Ganey survey results, a form sent to patients upon discharge. Helene blacked out staff names if the feedback wasn't positive. But the question of resources seemed like the kind of problem that couldn't be solved through gauze or surveys or suture trays.

When it was quiet—a forbidden word in the emergency department—I'd help with the billing. We'd break down charts as fast as possible: scan them, assign codes, and decide what to charge. Names I vaguely recognized flew by on the PDF reader. I studied my handwriting on their medication lists, a form techs weren't supposed to fill out but did anyway. (Nurses were supposed to keep up with the medication lists, but there was never enough time for them to actually do it.) Because there were only twenty slots on these forms, I sometimes had to use two pages.

I was twenty-three at the time, still paying off the cost of the mental-health-care debt I took on at nineteen, a cost I believed I would shoulder well into my thirties, a figure that felt more like a student loan than an appropriate cost for medical care. I didn't understand the nature of my mistake at the time, that I should have gone somewhere else for treatment—maybe the university hospital, where the state might pick up your bill if you were declared indigent, or nowhere at all. Sitting on a cot in the emergency room, I filled out paperwork certifying myself as the responsible party for my own medical care—signed it without looking, anchoring myself to this debt, a stone dropped in the middle of a stream. This debt was the cost of living, and I accumulated it in the telemetry unit, fifth floor, at a community hospital in Iowa City, hundreds of miles from home. There, I spent too much time playing with the plastic shapes that dangled from my IV line, which dripped potassium ions in carefully meted doses, like dimes from my future life funneled into a change-counting machine. I couldn't imagine the amount of money I'd spent—the debt I'd incurred—in attempting to end my life. *Suicide should be cheaper*, I remembered thinking. Probably half the costs were for psychiatry, for an illness it turned out I never really had. I was depressed, but a lot of people were depressed in college, it seemed. I only tried to kill myself after I began taking—and then stopped taking—all the medications I'd been prescribed, twenty-six in all. All for what turned out to be a vitamin deficiency, combined with hypothyroidism and a neurologically based developmental disorder.

And then there were the unintentional costs, those involving loss of work, lost friends, having to ask my father if he would drive to Iowa City and help me pack up all my belongings and move into a new apartment, since my roommate, who had also been diagnosed with mental illness, had developed a profound depression and moved out. He wanted to drive to Mexico on a motorcycle. My life did not have space for motorcycles.

When my bill finally reached me, it wasn't itemized, just "balance forwarded" from the hospital to the collection agency, after my paltry insurance covered the initial cost. From then on, I'd get calls requesting that I boost my payments, or I'd call them to switch bank accounts and they'd harass me on the phone. They would call me on my cell phone while I was at work, in the car, at home, in between shifts at the hospital, which I sometimes worked back-to-back if I could. For a long while I ignored them. I blocked their number, refused to answer when they dialed. My debt was five figures, an immense sum for someone making only $12.50 an hour. My coworkers in the ER were largely sons and daughters of first-generation immigrants. Most of them lived with their parents, and made up for it by driving nice cars. I lived in a third-floor walk-up almost far enough away from Iowa City to forget how much money I owed and to whom.

At the hospital where I worked, patients returned again and again, a kind of catch-and-release program, we joked, so nobody would pay for these stays. Some insurance plans prevented payment—as a kind of penalty—to hospitals that readmitted patients who'd been discharged inside thirty days. No payment to the hospital to disimpact a cognitively disabled ninety-eight-year-old woman, or to start two IVs and admit a woman who, at 108, had explained to the techs in providing her medical history that she had lost one of her older brothers in "the War," in a trench in France in 1917. The government thought that these people should have been cured, explained in hundreds of pages on the Centers for Medicare & Medicaid Services website, then later in the documents that made their way across Helene's desk. How do you explain the cost of a perennially septic patient whose nursing-home status and inconsistent care meant we'd see her again next month?

The patients who appeared on my screen flashed in bits and pieces, their visits reduced to minor explanations, to ICD-9 codes used to categorize their illnesses or injuries. I'd use their chart to determine what they should pay. If we were in doubt, we were expected to bill up (though this was never explicitly discussed)—that is, if someone received medical care from a physician assistant or other "midlevel" provider, the patient's care might cost less; but if the physician assistant or a nurse practitioner did more work (sutures, for example), the care could still get bumped up a level.

Suicide attempts were particularly resource dependent. Patients were admitted to a medical floor—perhaps the ICU—to deal with the physical costs of their attempts. Later, they transferred to psychiatry inpatient—nicknamed Fort Knox, as it was locked—after they had stabilized. The attempters came in sporadically, surprises tucked into the low points of our afternoons, beside admissions of women who had inexplicable feminine bleeds, and elderly men who slipped off sidewalks and into the street on sunny days. The attempters were people with conviction, but who lacked the ability to follow through. Who could blame them for their ineptitude, considering they wanted to do it at all?

There were rules in charging patients for emergencies, unique explanations for one billing code instead of another. If someone was discharged from an inpatient floor, she might find a toothbrush marked $8, an IV bag marked $25. In the emergency department, we assigned a level based on the type and duration of care, rather than itemizing each treatment individually, a complex algorithm based on many factors, but usually distilled into a few questions: Was the patient treated on the trauma or medical side of the ER? Sutures or no sutures? Cardiac workups? EKGs? Each level had its own exacting specifications, a way of making sense—at least financial sense—of the labyrinthine mess of billing. There was a surcharge for the physician (it was cheaper if they saw the physician assistant instead), and assorted charges for interventions, for the trappings of emergency—bandages, braces, Ortho-Glass for splinting. There was an expectation that you moved as quickly as you could. Hopefully you did not commit any errors along the way.

How much should it cost to put staples in a child's head? Staples seemed complicated. We weren't supposed to use anesthesia. It sounds like an act of unspeakable cruelty, but the truth of the matter is that people have less sensation in their scalps than in other parts of the body. The staple guns were autoclaved or thrown out after use; there were only so many staples available per gun. We stocked the ones that held fifteen or else twenty, and usually two or three or four did the job. Shafiq, the physician assistant I worked with most days, liked to mix a local, topical anesthetic—lidocaine-epinephrine-tetracaine, or LET—for children who came in needing staples. I loved the sharp smell of LET when I mixed it. The chemical reaction meant it started to work immediately after mixing, so I assembled the ingredients in front of the patient, stirred with the wooden end of a long cotton swab, which I then flipped and dipped into the solution to apply the gel. It reminded me of chemistry lab, of the courses in community college I liked best—black table-tops, wooden stools, a type of precision. In the meantime, the patient sat and bled on the cot. And then we waited until the anesthetic had done its job.

In patient charts, the LET sometimes bumped up the level of care. We asked patients' parents if it'd be okay if we used a little numbing gel for the child's scalp, and of course everyone said yes—yes, yes, yes. For us, this was tantamount to asking someone if they'd like elective cough syrup, or an aspirin, or some small gesture.

There were other costs. Dermabond was expensive—it was for open wounds, just superglue used to adhere flaps of skin back into place. We gave small stuffed toys to children who wouldn't stop crying in the ER, and although someone donated those toys, the time we spent stocking them meant that they cost as much as any other type of equipment we might use. Even the inexpensive things could be counted as a potential place to stem waste: sandwiches consumed by diabetics or (more likely) hungry techs, the little packages of cookies we used to placate toddlers whose siblings had been brought in. The boy on the bicycle, hit by a bus, whose blood was drawn twice because it clotted in the lab. A man in a C-spine collar, strapped to a back-board, off to X-ray for expensive films.

Helene told us everything was expensive; to be careful. Not everyone needed an EKG, or blood cultures, though that was usually a physician's problem, not a tech's responsibility. One of our docs only worked weekends and alternating holidays, brought doughnuts for the nurses—sugar placated even the angriest among us, the most difficult—and drew blood cultures on everybody over the age of fifty-five, which felt like just about everyone we ever saw. Helene seemed to speak to him without ever actually speaking to him—this guy who swooped into our hospital on a part-time, just-a-few-shifts-a-month basis, and spent money our hospital didn't have. I saw the waste in the cultures we'd draw on patients who inevitably were septic, others who were going to be discharged and thus would not need blood cultures, which took days to grow in glass bottles. By the time the blood cultures had grown, the patients would be long gone. It was like banding birds, a doc told me once. Still, I'd flick the lids off the bottles with my thumb, stick the patient's vein with a butterfly or straight needle, puncture the lid of the culture bottle with the needle attached to the other end of the tubing, and fill them to the appropriate line. Drawing blood bumped billing up a level. Cultures, even more.

These patient charts, the ones we broke down, were the happy endings in our emergency department. These were the patients who went home, who had someplace to go, who left the hospital alive and in good condition. Patients who died flashed up on our screens occasionally, but those were easy to bill: level five, the most expensive, as we would have performed "heroic measures" to try to save them. The lifesaving stuff was always exorbitant: The techs lined up to do CPR, two large-bore IVs, one in each arm, using what the paramedics called the coffee straw—an enormous needle. An EKG, or two, or three. An X-ray. And sometimes, depending on the nature of the illness, the cardiac cath lab, where a group of physicians, a nurse, and a scrub tech would thread the patient's arteries with a needle.

At nineteen, I needed a Helene for living, a responsible party who could have told me, You don't need to do this. That there were cheaper or better options than ending one's life. Instead, I swallowed 8,000 milligrams of lithium carbonate, received a gastric lavage and activated charcoal, then ended up on a monitoring floor, which added to the expense. From there, I was transferred to the psychiatric ward, where we spent all our time in the dayroom. When I left, I told everyone how it wasn't every place you could start your day with *The Carol Burnett Show*, but really all I could think about was what this treatment was going to cost me for years to come.

This thought, this recollection of the hospitalization, the subsequent bills, the cost of the ambulance to drive my unconscious body across town, the now fading first-name basis with the guy (Jeff? Or was it Ted?) ultimately assigned to my account, in collections, was something that came up—briefly, repeatedly, stunningly—whenever I worked in billing, like a bee sting. There was the prick of remembering, the wash of sudden insight. How responsible, how careful were we? Did I make a mistake in the last chart? Could I go back and revise? There was the guilt of billing a patient for too much—and we knew so many of these bills would never be paid, especially when there was no insurance to bill. Self-pay, we called them. You'd see it on the first page, upper right-hand corner, a mark against their futures. If I had a question, I could ask one of the two dedicated billers for our department. But then I'd start to recognize the handwriting as my own. Had I really put in for that test at the physician's request? And it cost how much?

Shafiq seemed to be one of the few in the department aware of the costs we assigned to our patients. He routinely cleaned and returned suture kits to patients and taught them how to remove their own stitches. We'd just throw away the tweezers anyway, and this way we could save the patient a trip back to the ER to get those sutures removed. "Nah, it's not a big deal," he'd say to the patient, handing him the tools. "Just take 'em out. Don't cut yourself." Shafiq had paid $50 per credit hour to finish his degree in Physician Assistant Studies at a community college on Chicago's West Side. He viewed himself as practical. Shafiq spoke endlessly about how basic medical care should be free, how we were "hosing everyone" by charging for LET, for staples, for particular levels of care. What if we were to treat everyone equally? What then?

At some point I started billing differently. I can't say when. It could have been when we had a patient die and I had to bill his family. It could have been when I saw the dizzying costs that were itemized for inpatient bills, or the time the woman I evaluated—my patient, our patient—and then billed was saddled with an amount she could never hope to pay. I remember her: how she came in and explained that things were difficult, that she didn't have insurance, but she needed someone to lance the boil that had erupted at her waistline. It had been causing her incredible pain, to the point where she could no longer dress herself. Please, she said. But she had already been registered, been given an ID bracelet, all the apparatuses of the emergency department and its tracking. Her bill popped up later on my screen; I saw the amount. This, somehow, totaled the cost of living. I thought of my own unpaid medical debt, reduced the amount, told no one, and let the next chart flash across my screen.

✧ ✧ ✧

Every December, I buy a cake for my second birthday: another year I'm still alive. Some years it's a cupcake; other years I opt for a grocery-store sheet cake. I invite friends over, or I have dinner with my husband and we sit and talk about work. I say that I've bought a cake. "Great," he says. He loves surprise cake. He doesn't know.

Recently, my bank was bought by another bank. This would

not be a notable fact except that I have been banking there since shortly after I was born. Before that, my parents banked there, and in the very early days of the institution, my aunt worked there as a teller. I modeled as a child, and I would endorse the checks from my earnings while lying on the floor of the bank, whose green carpeting hasn't changed in more than thirty years. When the bank relocated down the street, everything remained the same. I still know all the tellers and the personal bankers, the vice president, the president, Rodney, who works in the basement, reconciling transactions, I swear, with a red pencil. Any of them could look at my account and see that a collection agency had been debiting money on the twenty-fifth of the month, and had been doing so for almost ten years.

But the routing numbers changed with the acquisition, and so I called the collection agency to find out what had to be done. Perhaps I could give them a new routing number over the phone. Perhaps I would have to send them a canceled check. The company had offices in Iowa and Illinois, but the number was from Iowa, where I had been hospitalized. For years, upon seeing an Iowa number flash on my screen, I didn't pick up, just sent the calls to voicemail: my Iowa landlord, my friends, old coworkers, bosses, professors, and once, admission to graduate school. Now dialing the number felt strange.

The woman on the other end of the phone explained that the call may be recorded, that she was a debt collector and was attempting to collect a debt, the phrasing of federal law. Her voice was Iowa, flat vowels of the upper Midwest. "You know you've been paying this debt for a long time," she said.

"I know," I said. The conversation usually went something like this. So long, so much money. Usually debt collectors have to harass people on the phone, but not me, not anymore. I had fallen into line, paid the minimum every month on autopay. Twenty-five dollars a month times how many years equaled a bed in a monitoring floor.

"It's beyond the statute of limitations."

"Excuse me?" I was sitting at my father's desk. My husband and I had bought a house nearby, and we had begun to inherit all the stuff of aging parents. I had the new checks in my hand, the new checkbook. I rubbed my thumb on its pleather case. My chest felt full of the sterile strips we used to pack wounds: yards and yards of knit-cotton ribbon crammed into the cavity left by a lanced boil or pustule. The silence pooled larger and larger. I said nothing.

"If you were to stop paying it, nobody would be able to go after you, and it wouldn't show on your credit report."

I waited. "So I can stop paying it?" I asked.

"I'll remove your autopay information from my computer. Have a great weekend," she said, and hung up.

And then I did, too. I held the phone in my hand. It couldn't be right: they would call back in five minutes, or ten, or next week, or next month, when the payment was due, but nobody did.

❖ ❖ ❖

These days, I work far away from patients, writing up results of clinical trials or else abstracts for scientific congresses. The patients appear to me as raw data, depersonalized ID numbers, or in graphs that depict the efficacy of a particular drug, or as a way to explain value: One drug may cost more than another drug, but it is more useful, or requires fewer doses. The patients are further away—an idea, an endgame, a target hard to reach. All the work I do—the abstracts, the manuscripts, the slide decks—is in support of one drug, the next blockbuster, they call it. We are expensive, us medical writers. When I freelance for an agency, I bill by the quarter hour—like attorneys, or psychiatrists—and I think of Helene, her voice in my head. I try only to use what is necessary. But what, exactly, is necessary?

I Stalked My Psychiatrist

Even now, I adjust the image in my head, the term. Not stalked. *Researched*, I prefer to say. I knew where she lived and how many children she had. When she got a divorce, and the kids' names and ages appeared in the court records, I got a tingle of glee, just for knowing, which made me feel a little sick. My heart sped as I scrolled through those records or ones from the county recorder's office online. Available for anyone to see, I told myself. Public records.

I was seeing Dr. Smith—Julie, I called her later—because I had bipolar disorder, she claimed, and maybe something more drastic and dark, like a smidge of a personality disorder. Mental illness tended to run in my family the way kudzu covered everything south of the bug line. I wondered if I had some illness: anything to explain my way of existing in the world. But that was later. For now, I was sick and in need of care.

✧ ✧ ✧

According to Robert Muller, PhD, professor of psychology at York University, and the author of *Trauma and the Avoidant Client*, there are five kinds of stalkers. They are overwhelmingly male, lack skills to negotiate basic social interaction, and frequently stalk their victims as an act of revenge. The victims are overwhelmingly female, like my psychiatrist. The types include, in order of ascending creepy magnitude: rejected suitors, intimacy seekers, socially incompetent stalkers, resentful or revenge seekers, and predatory stalkers. Most stalker fantasies include intimacy or violence. They're mostly of average to above-average intelligence, tend to be well educated, and just over a fifth of them stalk due to mental illness or related factors; the rest do it out of anger or for retaliation or control, and they are incredibly good at rationalizing away inappropriate behaviors. Women are far less likely to stalk; when they do, it's with the hope of increased intimacy, erotomania, or with a hope for friendship. Maybe that one was me.

Julie was tall and beautiful and thin in a way that would suggest future osteoporosis, with auburn hair that reached her shoulders. She wore bright colors with sandals whenever possible, and for the most part seemed strong and practical and stubborn—a firstborn child, like me, but with a silly streak, as evidenced in toes dabbed with pink or blue or green nail polish. Most strangely of all, she seemed to like me. Here, she said, offering me a prescription, then sent me to book an appointment with a therapist.

I'm not sure where it started. The furnace. The dishwasher in its final cycle. The TV turned down so you couldn't make out the words people were saying. The guy on the radio with a lisp. I had seen a number of mental-health professionals over the years, starting at three when I banged my head against the floor for hours at a time. My mom thought I was either brain-damaged or on my way, so she took me to the pediatrician, and then to a children's social worker, who said I was encountering difficulty adjusting to the birth of my brother. Then I was too odd for elementary school, then secondary school. I preferred books as company to the companionship of people, wore comfortable clothes instead of what everyone else was wearing, found eye contact invasive at best. I slept with stuffed animals, struggled with waking up, with transitions of any kind. My mom dressed me every morning until fourth grade, when I changed schools again, and school started late enough I could mostly get myself together on time. I had always been different somehow. When I did connect with someone, it was usually an adult several times my age. Julie seemed to get me right away.

She had an abrasive sense of humor. When I asked about side effects for one of the many medications I would come to take, she said, "You know, the usual. Coma, death, developing the head of a golden retriever, sausage fingers . . ."

"Sausage fingers?"

"Yeah, you gotta watch out for those," she said, smirking. Inside everything lay the possibility for humor, for snark. Sarcasm was our method of relation, the way things made sense. She did things I had never seen other psychiatrists do, like slurp Diet Coke from a giant plastic cup on her desk or wear scarves she had clearly knit herself, scarves with the edges left unbound, a string dangling from each end. She had a tendency to let her glasses slip down her nose, like mine did, and put up giant quilts she pieced and sewed herself on the walls of her office. I saw her more frequently than I saw any other human in my life, and she remained a constant for over five years.

What's more, I liked her. I trusted her.

And I took twenty-six different medications while under her care. I didn't behave as expected when I took them; nothing seemed to "fix" me—so she switched one for another, over and over again. Often, I'd be the one to ask for another option. I was sensitive to everything and didn't like the side effects, of which there were many. Lithium made me nauseated and didn't seem to alleviate much of anything. Perphenazine made me chew my tongue ragged, and the antipsychotics all made me feel crazier than I was before I began taking medication at all, locked in a swimmy, cotton-brained confusion. When I tried to talk to her about it, she seemed distant. You'll adjust, she explained. But I didn't.

More than anything, I was bad at describing what was happening to me. Newly adult and expected to shop for my own groceries, I struggled with the noise and the color in the grocery store and what to buy once inside. Frequently, I came back with the wrong things, or nothing at all. I didn't have an eating disorder; I'd just get inside the grocery store and my stomach would flip-flop at the low drone of fluorescent lights, the intensity of the citrus display. And food frequently changed locations within the store. If they moved something from an endcap where I'd found it the week before, it would take me hours to find it again. I'd wander the aisles in a daze, hoping to get something to eat. For weeks I lived on grape juice and Triscuit, or bananas, or string cheese, or prepackaged lunch meat. I knew how to cook. I was an excellent cook, had worked as a pastry chef's assistant during high school. But grocery shopping was a baffling, dizzying experience, so I avoided it whenever possible.

I became obsessed with driving. It had taken me a long time to learn, and I wanted to make up for it by driving as much as possible. I cast loops around town, putting thousands of miles on my car without ever leaving the state. And with little to do between occasional school attendance, feeding horses, and attending *medication management* appointments, as Julie called them, I found myself driving on the main road by her house. Or her old house, as by then, she'd started the process of getting divorced from her husband and had all but moved in with another psychiatrist in her office. I saw them at my early morning appointments, looking guilty and freshly showered. Just one car parked behind their office, I noticed. So I memorized her car, his truck, her ex-husband's car. Then I started driving near the new house.

When they bought that house, I knew almost immediately how much they paid for it through public records online. When the house went on the market, later, I clicked through the pictures, fascinated by the colors: a blue bathroom, a cantaloupe kitchen, the forest green dining room. I scrolled through the pages on the ad, trying to justify her choices. I was working as a real estate assistant, too, so I rationalized away the experience of looking up Julie's information. And because I worked in the same office as her listing agent and my boss had another listing across the street, I got to hear feedback, juicy tidbits on the colors, from those who had shown the listing, even going so far as to tell Julie, though I never told her I knew it was her house. I was a knitter and made quilts. I fantasized about how it would have been if we had met under other circumstances, like in a quilters' group.

I never wanted her to actually see me outside the office. When I coincidentally ran into her and her daughter at the grocery store in our small college town, I ducked into another aisle and pretended to be fascinated by the rows of jarred pickles or canned tuna fish to avoid even the possibility of interaction. I wanted to feel close, to connect in some way that wasn't possible.

I don't know what I was looking for. Even now it feels strange and horrid to me; not me. In the meantime, the drugs started piling up, each more debilitating than the one before. Saphris was sublingual, slipped under the tongue, and sounded beautiful but left an acrid taste in my mouth, made me feel subhuman, like my thoughts weren't even my own. Zyprexa drowned me, a swimming pool slowly filled to the brim, the chlorinated smell sharp on my nose. I still thought of Julie as friendly, helpful. I'd argue about taking the drugs, stop taking them, start taking them—I was a terrible patient—but ultimately tried my best to do whatever she said. I wanted to do the right thing, even if she didn't always seem right.

The first indicator that she might not be right came after a discussion we had about Facebook. "People say you're 'friends' with them on Facebook, but Facebook friends aren't real friends," I complained. After the appointment, I found her profile, new and mostly unlocked, under her maiden name, and filled with pictures of her weekends with the new psychiatrist husband, drinking at Jimmy Buffett concerts, smiling, laughing with other similarly aged people. *Parrotheads*. At the following appointment, I suggested that she talk to her children about how to make sure her profile was friends only. She blanched, wide-eyed, stared at me, quiet for a minute, then recovered. "Of course," she said, an edge to her voice, and immediately the photos were gone again.

Sometimes she was caustic, bitter. She asked me to be her guinea pig, told me that she had gotten these drug samples for free and could I let her know what I thought of them? The guinea pig part was a joke, I thought, but wasn't sure. I wasn't always the best at figuring out whether or not someone was joking. But there was a sweetness, a humanness, too: Early on, she'd seemed to speak my language, took my hand to lead me down the street to the hospital when the depression settled heavy and flat across my chest. We took the stairs instead of the elevator because I couldn't figure out what expression to make with my face if we were to share the elevator with other people in the hospital. So she walked up four flights of stairs with me instead.

Years into our psychiatric relationship, I went to see a neuropsychologist at the suggestion of my therapist. "You might have a learning disability," I was told. I had some vague recollection of an ADD diagnosis as a kid, and hoped that maybe there would be some sense to the strangeness about me, how I missed all the social cues, how I felt so irritable and brittle all the time. *Brittle*—that was a word the neuropsychologist would use, but it felt right to me. I spoke too quickly—my speech came from a pressurized can—made inappropriate or nonexistent eye contact, and had a tendency to talk in circles when nervous. And then there was the depression, like a dark and suffocating foam. I had tried all the drugs and nothing worked.

The neuropsychologist determined I had anxiety and something called nonverbal learning disability, a neurological developmental disability with components similar to autism, not bipolar disorder. The depression likely came from a vitamin D deficiency and untreated hypothyroidism made worse by the addition of lithium. So I started taking medication for my thyroid, and vitamins. Dropped the rest. Felt better. And stopped following Julie altogether.

Some time after I stopped seeing her, I requested my records. I flipped through them, startled by her descriptions of me: Was this the way to explain myself to myself? What had I done? I was "casually dressed," or "on time," or "WNL"—code for "within normal limits." It made me think of a long-distance trucker with two logbooks: one for the police, and one of what really happened. But what really happened?

Now, years later, when I think of having followed her, I'm seasick. Julie never said anything to me about it and may not have even been fully aware. I mentioned that I had looked up information about her online to my therapist, who was in the same office, and she reminded me, of course, that that was not a good idea. That it gave a false sense of intimacy, or created an environment that wasn't real or true. Like the stalkers I read about, I thought—what Dr. Muller described as the intimacy seekers or the socially incompetent—and I wondered if I was one of them. So I read memoirs of psychiatrists who had been stalked. Was this me? I asked myself, flipping the pages.

But the truth is, I don't know the truth. Don't know if maybe

I could have been crazy and just resistant to all those drugs she prescribed, that in trying to design a life for myself I missed out or forgot about the times when the drugs worked. Might have driven past, or not driven past, any number of places I admit to now. There were differences in my behavior at times—and I could attribute those to certain drugs, maybe. But I could just as easily attribute them to something else. In a sense, all those hundreds of visits and hundreds of pages of records I requested—trying to make sense of the person I was at the time—may or may not mean anything at all.

I looked Julie up recently after years of forgetting. Wanted to know if she was still practicing, and where. They moved their practice to a new building across town. Still doing the same thing she did before, in fifteen- or twenty- or thirty-minute increments, tens of times a day. Just beneath the link in the search results for her new office, her new last name, her new practice, was a review from another former patient: "She just wanted to give me more drugs." Me too, I wanted to tell the former patient, but instead I closed my laptop and went outside to sit in the sun.

Clipped

The year I applied to college, my parents made $19,867.85.

It seemed so low that I went back through the online form again and double-checked my math. I knew this because I did their taxes in order to qualify for financial aid, though the first time I tried, I filled out the FAFSA with all zeroes instead of their social security numbers, because my father refused to supply this information to the federal government. What business of theirs was it, he would ask, and I tried to explain that my scholarship was tied to this information, but he wouldn't budge. My parents hadn't been convinced of the value of my attending college, and I wasn't sure either. I could go to dog-grooming school—I already had a job at PetSmart, washing dogs—and make a good living, or I could be a waitress, because I could pour and was good at remembering things. Maybe write in my spare time.

We lived in a side-by-side duplex just east of town, and rented out one side and lived in the other half. Legally, it was a two-unit town house, but this only became a problem later, when my parents lost half of it to their former tenant, who stopped paying rent and picked it up for pennies on the dollar at a foreclosure auction. Each side of the duplex was enormous, over five thousand square feet, built for two sisters who wanted to live next to each other. It was called the Double House, built in 1886, and was on the state register of historic places. My father had unfailingly, slowly replaced the rough sawn cedar siding that had been put up in the 1970s with historically accurate Dutch lap and narrow quarter-sawn fir siding; the house was then painted

in historic gray and white, with blue-gray doors. There was a
meticulousness to everything he did, and mostly it showed up
in the house we made and how we lived. It meant that there was
not much room for deviation, but at the same time, we were all
constantly deviating, about to run off the road, to lose control.
My father had grown up in conditions that were best described
as extraordinary poverty and abuse, and so imbued in him was
both a frantic urge to make a lot of money and the tendency to
spend it all before anyone else did. This was how we operated,
in a constant churn of being flush with money and then broke-
ish. What I mean by this is that my father drove a Land Rover
and decreed that only a certain brand of toilet paper would
enter our house, but then recklessly remortgaged the house to
pay for my brother's boarding-school tuition or else failed to
pay the electric or the gas bill. The vacuum cost $500, and we
had three of them, one for each floor.

Most days I worked at PetSmart, in the grooming department, where $9 an hour plus tips meant I could clear at least
$200 a week or more working part-time. First, the uniform:
black quick-dry pants that went *swish swish* when you walked,
black rubber-soled shoes, T-shirts, no visible facial piercings or
tattoos. Hair pulled back if it was long. Grooming smock, which
draped on my body like a sheet. This was the part of my life
where I was considered tall, still, and had no chest to speak of;
my hair was short, and I got sirred a lot, which wasn't an issue in
grooming. At school, everybody accused me of being a lesbian,
even though I had dated widely. I had not gotten the memo
regarding how to be a person. School was a coat that didn't
fit, much like the one I wore every day: long, wool, large, and
men's, worn no matter the season, with steel-toed black boots.
I was not expected to go to college because it was not expected
that I'd get in. Half my classmates believed I was going to shoot

up the place, like those Columbine kids when we were in middle school. The other half asked me for drugs because they thought I dealt.

My manager's name was Fran. She was from New York and had her real estate license, too, just in case. I feel now like maybe she was one of those secretly wealthy people, the kind you hear about later, donating millions of dollars to animal shelters, willing it away from ungrateful children who never visit because executive jobs on the East or West Coast keep them away. Fran struck me as *that kind of person*, like maybe she secretly owned half the apartment buildings in Waukegan, Illinois, and her net worth easily exceeded that of half her customer base at PetSmart. They thought of her as Fran, $5 or $10 tip, and she said, *Thank you very much, Mrs. Douglas, we'll see you next month, bye, Bitsy, or Bijou, or Molly, good dog.* Really she stuffed the money in her pocket and waited for them to leave before starting to complain.

"Did you see what she was wearing? Like, oh my gawd, *come on*," she said, all Brooklyn. She was a tough woman; you could see it in her squint; she could punch somebody out with just her eyelashes, which extended past her browline in a single murky sweep. If you'd washed a tip dog, she slipped the money into your smock between two manicured fingers after the customer ran out the door. "Thanks, hon, for washing Binky, or whatever the hell his name is," she said. "Shit, I need a cigarette," she said. "I am never doing her dog again," she said. "I don't care if that Mrs. Douglas tips me or whatever, did you see how he was climbing all over the table? He's totally matted and she always wants the same. *Oh, Fran, Please keep Binky long this time.* Brush your damn dog," Fran said, a little under her breath.

Of course, Fran had been doing Binky for years, it said so right in the computer, but nobody brought it up. Next month, when they called and said that only Fran can do the dog, that he's special, that he likes Fran, that he bit some other groomer, the man, he's not very good, is he—one of the girls would write *Binky Douglas, 2:00,* just like that.

Once Ivan and I got to know each other, he let me in on a little secret. "Grooming is shit job," he said. "Emmy, Emily, you go to college, yes." Ivan was a veterinarian and an attorney in his old country, Ukraine, and spoke Ukrainian, Russian, Polish, French, and English. His American customers couldn't understand a damn word he said. "You like short, yes?" he said. "I do, okay, very good," he said. Before the year was up, his wife and son moved back to Poland, where they lived before they came to the United States, leaving Ivan in their second-floor walk-up in Rogers Park, the empty bedroom made up for if and when his son visited.

At lunch, I read. I read pretty much whatever I could find: Vonnegut novels or short stories or the PetSmart canine grooming guidelines, a spare copy of which could be found in our break room. We, the groomers, were separate from the rest of the store. We did not have normal lunch breaks or fifteen-minute breaks; we worked eleven- or twelve- or fifteen-hour days because the groom shop made more money than all the other departments combined. Fran took care of us, like kids: she bought us lunch and had it delivered, or slipped us tip money for cigarettes or gum, or attended our alternative high school graduations, or tried to think of ways to convince my parents to let me get a dog. It wasn't allowed under any circumstances, so I didn't know why we tried, but whenever a Portuguese Water Dog puppy came in to be groomed, Fran snapped my photo with our Polaroid camera, me grinning and holding the dog. It was the perfect kind of dog for my parents: it had hair, not fur, didn't shed, liked to swim, was highly trainable. Initially the dog was denied because my brother was allergic, but Portuguese Water Dogs are hypoallergenic, I told my parents. They said no anyway; nobody wanted a dog but me.

I was at my seventh school in ten years. My mom moved me, because I didn't fit in, though it was more than that. I kept dropping out, working more, balanced on a thin edge of living. The reason why I moved always seemed to be shifting. My last school was Catholic, the one before that private, then two public schools before that, another Catholic school, another public school. My mother and I were not getting along: she was going through menopause as I underwent puberty. We spent a lot of time screaming at each other.

I knew something was wrong, that maybe there was a fire and everyone was inside the house. Everything was difficult: I'd sit down to do homework, for once, get up for a glass of water, and the homework would be recycled by the time I got back. There was a drug drawer in our kitchen in case you needed a pick-me-up—Vicodin from my mother's dentist or weed or some other things. My mother's filing system meant you could find socks in the refrigerator on any day of the week.

✧ ✧ ✧

The schedule at the new school was fine except for Honors English, which I didn't plan on taking. "Listen," I told the registrar, "do I have to take this class?" I pointed to my schedule. "Right here. Right before lunch. I don't think Honors English is such a good idea," I said, frowning. Hadn't I taken enough English classes already? I thought about transferring to the alternative high school, where my friend Jane from grooming took night classes.

Jane was there because she couldn't seem to make it to class during the day. She was a Deadhead, all dreadlocks and patchouli, an only child who lived with her parents in a little ranch house away from the road, where they grew pot in their greenhouse. In truth, I had my GED, got it through the library when I was fourteen, but my parents were making me go to high school anyway. "GEDs are for pregnant teenagers," my dad said. I was working on becoming an emancipated minor, too.

"Sorry," the registrar said, handing my schedule back to me. "If we do that we have to bump your math class down a couple of levels, and"—she looked at the computer—"we can't. You know, you scored in the ninety-eighth percentile in math," she said.

I didn't know this, but I nodded anyway. Maybe I wouldn't come to school before lunch.

✧ ✧ ✧

"Emily," my mother said. "If you smoked just a little bit of pot every day, just a puff or two, I think you'd feel a lot better."

We stood in the kitchen: my mother's design. There were four sinks, three ovens, two dishwashers, a wok, a grill, and a commercial Northland-brand refrigerator that hummed like an aircraft carrier. The countertops were laboratory grade. We spent a lot of time telling visitors that you could pour acid on them, but nobody ever asked for a demonstration. We would lose this house eventually, but not until I got to college.

We had had this conversation before, about the weed. She would buy it for me, she said. The good stuff.

I didn't think it made much difference if the weed was *good* or not, at least not to me. I was too much of a rule follower anyway; even the idea of doing something illegal felt absurd. I was interested in order, in black and white, even though nearly everything was gray at home and otherwise. There were too many boundaries or not enough: I had worked at a bakery before PetSmart, as a pastry chef's assistant and also in the front of the store, where they occasionally offered a Swiss coffee service and stale pastries that didn't make it out the door to their wholesale business. There were too many moving pieces, not enough math to make sense of the world in which we lived. At the bakery, I could walk to work, but only made $5.15 an hour. At PetSmart, I made $9, but I had a commute to work that was only ameliorated by my friend driving, or else my friend's mom; I had not yet gotten my license because I couldn't get anyone to practice with me. What if I needed a new job, one that required drug testing?

✧ ✧ ✧

After school, my math teacher invited me to go over problems with her. She said "invited," but she really meant that she'd rather I came up with some kind of explanation for my grades in math instead of lying to her about how I didn't get it. "You are kind of a mystery," Mrs. Gilbert said, because I could do the problems for math team but couldn't figure out regular old precalculus for the purposes of her class. Basically, I was terrible at addition. "I have two questions," she said. "One, why do you get the hard problems but not the easy ones?" I didn't say anything; I had a feeling that this was rhetorical. "Two, do you want to join the math team?" I couldn't because of the groom shop, because of my hours, because of work. "Nah, it's not for me," I said, but I would have done anything to join.

I spent a lot of time thinking about how my life could be different. College sounded absurd, but my English teacher was insistent.

In class, our first day, he was impressed by my Radclyffe Hall reference. He said so, writing me a note afterward, something like, *Emily, I was really impressed by your Radclyffe Hall reference.* This was the beginning of the end, I thought.

When I wasn't at school or at work, I was seeing several psy-
chologists. I had been hospitalized for a brief, forty-eight-hour
period in June that year. I'd just turned seventeen; everything
felt heavy and impossible. School had let out and I'd spent a lot
of time at home, waiting for my summer job schedule to start.
Because I had told her I was planning on killing myself, my
mother had checked me in to a locked adolescent ward at a sub-
urban hospital two towns over. I spent two days there, the rest of
the week in intensive outpatient therapy, and then was quickly
released: the feeling had passed. This was something I'd come
to believe, with time, ran in our family, a darkness that couldn't
be eased or eliminated. The prescription for Lamictal, an anticonvulsant, had stayed, though it didn't seem to make much of
an impact on how I felt or what I was doing. I just needed to get
out of the house, before it killed me.

By fall of my senior year, at PetSmart, things were more or
less the same. We worked fifteen-hour days, because the holidays were coming up and everybody needed to *make plan* which
meant that we had sales-goal figures that sounded outrageous,
because they were. Here was the routine: In the back, where no
customer went, we ran out of kennels, so we tied dogs to each
other, dogs to the floor, the tubs, the kennels, ourselves. We
eagerly waited for two dogs from the same family to come in,
which meant we could tie their leashes together and wash them
at the same time, get them done faster, and faster, and get them
out the door. We called all our customers to see if we could get
them to come in late on a Saturday night, because the week was
ending and we were just a few bucks short. Jane and I compared
battle scars: our fingers lost their feeling, and then there was
the rash. We called them "lobster claws," because your forearms
turned red, then your hands, then your fingertips, from being

up to your elbows in shampoo all day. My skin flaked off in sheets.

Later that fall, Ivan tried to sell me on the idea of attending college again.

We sat across from each other in folding chairs in the PetSmart break room. He was trying to find out how much public universities cost, because some kind of economic model might get me to change my mind, since it wasn't that expensive to go to a state school. He didn't know that my parents had made $19,867.85 the previous year, or that my dad had been holed up in his upstairs office playing chess on the computer, caught in some perpetual unemployment, one where he barely left the house, or that my mom kept offering to buy me drugs to *even me out a little* in hopes that she could use them, too (her eyes said she was hoping for opium, her drug of choice, but would settle for plain old marijuana), or that we just *seemed* outwardly normal, we seemed like these upper-middle-class people living some kind of upper-middle-class life. Ivan thought I was saving the money I made at PetSmart for college, but most weeks we cashed my check to pay for groceries.

"Oh, sure, college sounds great," I said, lying into my pastrami on rye. I tried to talk myself out of it: I wasn't really the academic sort, I didn't have time to attend school because of work, everyone kind of assumed I was a moron anyway. But I'd go, eventually. My parents would find the money for me to attend school—from where, I couldn't say—and I would apply and pay the $30 application fee with a check I wrote and mailed to the school. I'd fill out the FAFSA and guess at the numbers they wanted; in subsequent years I'd sneak through my parents' files and memorize their social security numbers so I could put together the form. This was how things would come together. Ivan rubbed his tongue over dark teeth.

"If I can do, you can do," he said. He crumpled the butcher paper from his sandwich and tossed it into the trash can. "Emmy, you listen, I am pretty smart guy, eh?" He tapped his index finger against his temple.

"Let's go wash dogs," I said.

Some Therapy

There were twelve before Julie.

1. The play therapist I saw as a toddler, when I was having trouble adjusting to the birth of my brother, and then trouble adjusting to school. The play therapist and I played with trains, sitting on the floor in her cool loft office in downtown Oak Park, Illinois. She cost several hundred dollars an hour, I'm sure.

2. The elementary school social worker who thought that there might be something wrong with me. She was concerned that I described my parents' jobs the way I did, that they worked real estate brokerage and development, how it seemed irregular. How I missed a lot of school, that my parents weren't keen on attending parent-teacher conferences. How I'd learned to forge my mother's signature for releases or forms. I was modeling, mostly commercial print, had an agent in the city. This, too, was hard for the social worker to understand. Her sessions were free, but it was about a thousand dollars a year for the parish school.

3. In middle school, the social worker in private practice who wanted to evaluate me for medication, maybe ADHD, because I didn't fit in and my grades were poor at my private K–8 Country Day school. I thought squash was a vegetable, but it turned out to be a game. Everything seemed to be coded in a way I didn't understand. My oddness

manifested itself in being unable to decipher the back-and-forth of conversation, not knowing how far away to stand from people, my tendency to interrupt, my entire room full of horse figurines in a middle school of class-mates who talked about music and boys. The collections of stones and stamps and birds' nests: anything animal related would do. The hundreds of books I'd devour every summer instead of playing with the kids in the neighborhood. We had health insurance, then, through Blue Cross and Blue Shield of Illinois, but mental health wasn't covered.

4. There was the licensed counselor whose name and face I can't remember, though her office felt sterile and gray. She referred me to the pediatric neurologist, who cost four hundred dollars.

5. My father's psychiatrist, Dr. J. Bornstein, a man who had tardive dyskinesia, the shakes, from OD'ing on Zoloft in the early nineties. My father took Zoloft, too, then, start-ing when I was nine; it kept him in check somehow, let the anger and anxiety leach from his body instead of screaming at me. I was the oldest and the only girl and being raised to assume certain responsibilities, mostly having to do with cleaning and taking care of the house and its occupants, items that weren't part of my brothers' purview, and I hated this role. Dr. Bornstein continued to take Zoloft, too, because the thing that nearly killed him also kept him alive; my father saw him for nearly twenty years. I saw the evidence in my father's checkbook, a few hundred dollars at a time. Dr. Bornstein called me "the Emmis," which is Yiddish for "the absolute truth,"

because of my tendency to be blunt and honest in everything I did.

6. I saw the pediatric neurologist in junior high, who said I had *developmental differences*. In the report that came back later, addressed to my father's psychiatrist, who must have also been involved, she detailed the ways in which I was different. How I couldn't tell right from left, my strange gait; she made recommendations for medication or therapy or ideally both. There could be other interventions, maybe some occupational or physical therapy, to remedy various issues. I wouldn't see the letter until over a decade later. My mother read it, claimed she said I *needed drugs*, which horrified her, and we never went back again.

7. The woman in Glencoe, a quiet North Shore suburb, who specialized in seeing adolescents in the evenings, thought me "unusual" because of my ability to solve the puzzles she left on her coffee table in a minute or two, and wanted to involve my mother in therapy together, which felt like a very specific nightmare. In session, my mom pointed out that the puzzles were easy to solve and thus not an example of anything.

8. The clinical psychologist in Evanston who had too many plants. I'd take the train to see her, past the shoe store full of sensible options, up the stairs or elevator to her office, where she wore the same shoes I saw in the window downstairs. She wanted us to bond, so sometimes we'd get lunch or something; she'd offer to buy me a hot dog at the stand around the corner and I'd politely decline. I didn't understand what she was doing; I didn't want to

be seen with her. Once, a classmate of mine appeared in her waiting room. Mutually horrified, we pretended we didn't know each other, and I stopped seeing Plant Lady shortly thereafter.

9. The licensed clinical social worker who fancied himself "cool." We talked a lot about politics and avoided discussing how a group of girls had started bullying me in the locker room before gym class or how my chem teacher, a man in his late twenties, would check me for track marks in front of the entire class (I wasn't a drug user) or how I was dating a woman and terrified my mother would find out. When she did find out, I wasn't allowed to see her anymore, and then I transferred schools again. The social worker's clients met him in a building that was part of a vacant office park adjacent to the bowling alley I'd been chased out of for looking too gay. It just felt like a lot to keep going there. Fifty dollars a session, after insurance.

10. Dr. P., the psychiatrist I saw after being hospitalized for a few days in high school for *suicidal ideation*. He would not make eye contact, instead writing orders facing away from me, sitting at his desk outside the adolescent unit where I'd just been discharged. My hospitalization in high school totaled tens of thousands of dollars. Insurance paid for some but not all of it.

11. The clinical psychologist who wanted to see me weekly after I'd been discharged from the hospital. I went once. She kept copies of *Highlights* magazine fanned out on a coffee table in her office waiting area. What could I even say?

12. The woman who operated out of a basement office in Iowa City, who cried during our sessions whenever I talked about my childhood. She seemed to be going through something. I gave this impression to some people, that it was okay for them to talk to me in this way. So I tried to be friendly and open, and attempted to help her with her problems. Then I stopped seeing her—the act of managing got to be too much. I paid her a hundred dollars at a time.

Sick

I have a close relationship with the upstairs bath. Specifically, its toilet. The dull *pinging-thump* of my fingernails against the side of its hollow body. The way I find my brain tracing our bathroom tile, slightly unfocused, as I retch. My medication is responsible for my body's daily transformation from sleeping person into the monster I become. The vomit erodes the enamel on my teeth, and my dentist thinks I have an eating disorder, even after repeated assurances to the contrary. In the early morning, the bathroom window sash rattles against the wind.

The upstairs bath is configured like a gun. The barrel makes up the hallway and bathtub, and as you walk farther in, the room unfolds a little: vanity, toilet; the linen closet performs the function of the hammer. The house was built before indoor plumbing, the bath added later, so nothing lines up properly, and the evidence is visible in the bathroom's proportions, or lack thereof. The wallpaper peels off the wall behind the sink like parchment infused with years of toothpaste spittle, and the medicine cabinet stands empty. From working in an emergency department at a busy hospital, I know I shouldn't keep medicine in the cabinet; it's too humid in there. In mine, there are Q-tips or small expired insects or arachnids or dental floss in a tin whose age is calculated by the quality of rust evident on its container.

Some mornings the room gets blurry and spins, and in the corner of my eye appears a flashlight's bulb. I think this is what seizures must resemble: this is what they mean to the body, all stimuli and no way of processing.

Lithium is a salt. It occupies space number three on the periodic table, a silver-white alkali metal, simpler than any of the salts with which our bodies are familiar. Sodium is a mere eight electrons away, but the quantity of energy necessary to change lithium into sodium is too vast to imagine, so they might as well be years' worth of electrons of difference. When I take my medication, lithium carbonate, I think of table salt, big square prisms of taste under a microscope, the edges shaved sharp as if by a knife. Sodium chloride. But the imagined other salt is not enough to make my actual medication palatable. Since the company that manufactures the pills no longer enteric-coats the extended-release version, the pills are chalky in my palm. Nightly, before bed, I complete a ritual: something to eat, something to drink, and then the pills. Two of them, little eyes staring up at me.

Five years of this stuff, and no end in sight.

I tell my friends I've been sick, and don't elaborate on the details. For them, sick is in bed with the flu. Sometimes I am explicit enough to say stomach flu. Rarely are they close enough a friend to explain that the source of my sickness is lithium.

The accidental overdose is hard to explain. People think that since I must be crazy, I must be somehow responsible for the explanation that comes with overdose most of the time: suicidality. And although, once, I took too much lithium on purpose, it is not the case here, every day. Maybe I am dehydrated when I complete the ritual, taking these pills, or have forgotten that I've taken them and double-dosed, or not timed my meals effectively enough; no matter. The results are the same. I can't go to the hospital for my vomiting, dehydration, chills, fever. I entertain the notion, briefly, think about it, in the upstairs bath, my forehead pressed against the toilet's porcelain tank. I live a mere three blocks from the hospital, just down the street, and I can see the ER waiting room from my front yard. It's not really an option, of course, but I consider it anyway. Going into the ER in the predawn hours is asking for it. Asking for something, anyway, something that likely turns into an involuntary admission to the psychiatric floors.

ER techs are taught not to believe anything that psychiatric patients say. This is good advice to heed in most situations: they lie. I try to explain it to my psychiatrist, Julie, who won't return my calls. She says I can just go to the ER because it's an emergency. But when I meet with her in person and explain, her face softens, just a bit, and I know she knows exactly what I mean.

The lithium metabolizes at a specific rate: the Paul Perry nomogram is a graph constructed by Dr. Perry some number of years ago, one that says the appropriate amount of lithium makes sense in number of millimeters per mol, 0.6 to 1.2. I've seen it once, in my chart, following a hospitalization, something about the patient, whose identity is tied to the values ascribed to the chart. I am supposed to take between 900 and 1350 milligrams daily. A mere 900 is on the low end according to blood draws, but I'm not sure what else to do, when even that is enough to make me sick. Later, I will find out that this is not the right dose for a lot of people. But the consequences of not taking it at all are somehow a hundred times greater.

These chalky, yellow pills in my palm. With them, I am not crippled by anxiety at the grocery store, unable to decide if I want lentils or split peas for soup. Wondering if I am worthy enough to buy bread today. I don't have to drive to faraway locales during hallucinatory episodes. There are no strangers in my bedroom, asking strange questions. Color is not associated with a particular sound or inflection. There is a natural order to things, an unspoken rhythm, coming together in carefully meted doses.

The man I will eventually marry doesn't understand. When I call to tell him I have lithium toxicity, he oohs in mock sympathy, unable to comprehend its severity. To him, psychiatric medications have side effects like dry mouth and sexual dysfunction. Lithium is considered the *gold standard* in cases like mine. Ori has taken something once, been prescribed antidepressants, but the effect they have on him is not the same as the effect on me: he gets happier, a little less morose, the chemical effect of fluoxetine. I tell him my problem is brain chemistry and his is just a moral failing. I take fluoxetine once, to see if it could maybe do better for me than the lithium, only to find a kind of blue mania, one unchecked by sleep.

I think about others who are in this same place, or have been here, in places like my bathroom, counting the bathroom tiles, waiting for the nausea to subside, the barometric pressure to rise a little, to regain the natural order of things. People wonder why illness is hard. My father shuffles around the house he shares with my mother, his slippers padding on the hardwood floors of the old Victorian rowhouse, the Double House. The Double House harbors a double life: one boxed by a therapeutic dose of Zoloft, a carefully dictated existence. But he can't hold on to that, he misses dreaming, and so he stops taking that therapeutic dose and shuffles around the house instead, refusing sandwiches assembled by my mother, invitations to walk the dogs. He stays inside instead, lives in fear of shampoo.

And then, it is nearly over. The planets of our bathroom realign into their respective orbits, Pluto included. The room stops spinning. Everything presses against the inside of my skull. I brush my teeth, find clean scrubs, and appear at the ER, for work, a care provider, an emergency room technician, a preceptor of new techs, a phlebotomist: well enough to pass, to make it look as though my presence is deliberate.

A
Brief Inventory
of My Drugs
and
Their Retail
Price

- Zoloft. This was always my father's medication, originally, a place he went to keep the ghosts at bay. Maybe, my father's psychiatrist said, I could try it, too, just to see if it would do the same for me. I took it for a week, when I was seventeen, then tried it again years later, when we'd reached the kitchen sink part of our treatment. It's been available as a generic since 2006; I would have taken the brand name, which averages $274 a month. Years later, I would work on a Zoloft ad campaign, the one with the depression cartoon, a mobile detailing app for physicians who were thinking about prescribing it and wanted to know how it held up to other drugs in its class. I made $25 an hour, freelancing for a health-care advertising agency, no health insurance, dispatched to an office park a forty-minute drive from my apartment. I ate lunch in my car every day.

- Seroquel. I first took this one in spring 2004, a few months into my treatment with Julie. She felt I wasn't sleeping enough. In truth, I had recently been hired to work at the Procter & Gamble plant, working third shift, screwing tops on shampoo bottles on the No. 11 line. We made Herbal Essences, mostly. I was hired for $10 an hour. The base hourly pay was $7.65, same as Walmart if you did the cake decorating, which I was also hired to do, but if you worked third shift at the factory, they gave you extra. *Hazard pay*, people said. It was the kind of place where sometimes accidents happened, and third shift was rife with them. I never went to work; instead I'd call off and sit in the park on the swings at midnight, panicking. I didn't know this was panic. I thought everything was fine, I just needed to work harder, to get my shit together. Why was living so much easier for everyone else? I couldn't tell her, not now, not ever. The 25 milligram tablets retail for $6.33 each.

- Thorazine. I didn't sleep. I can't even remember, but there it is, on my chart. $40.

- Gabapentin. It had a reputation in some circles for being a kind of snake oil. Years later, when I worked in the ER, I'd see gabapentin on someone's chart and inevitably one of the nurses or doctors or techs or all of us would roll our eyes, say something like *buckle up* or *you know what that means.* We all knew what it meant: that the patient had been taking this drug off-label, maybe for generalized pain or more likely for bipolar depression. It's supposed to be for seizures or neuropathic pain caused by shingles, but nobody we saw ever took it for that, not anymore. Some people took it for alcohol withdrawal, or anxiety, or essential tremors, or just as a placebo when nothing else worked. It's been generic for decades, so at least it was cheap: $5 a month, if I remember. I took it on and off, usually in combination with something else, for years.

- Wellbutrin. This was the drug my father came to take when the Zoloft stopped working. I got a free blister pack, the kind that came from Julie's locked Rubbermaid cabinet, to start. I took it for a week, maybe, then stopped; it felt like I wasn't me anymore. Getting off it was harder than getting on it. I loved the idea of it: that maybe I could take something common, well known, something that everyone in my classes was probably also on. I knew people who had taken it to stop smoking, or because they were a little depressed. It was the kind of drug that sometimes showed up in other people's medicine cabinets at parties. What a thrill. When I stopped taking it, everything showed up bright and harsh and intensely beautiful; I ground my teeth at night for a week. It retailed at the time for around $80 a month without insurance.

- Geodon. The little white bottle with the blue label; the pharmacist didn't even bother decanting it into an amber bottle at Walgreens, just slapped the label on top of the existing one. I remember placing it in my medicine cabinet after I had moved into a new apartment twenty miles from Iowa City, in the old Ford dealership building, across the street from the new Ford dealership and down the street from the Alibi Club, one of two bars in town, if you counted the VFW. My apartment had fifteen-foot ceilings because they used to park cars inside it. You had to pick up mail at the post office if you lived in town; USPS only delivered to rural routes. I was PO Box 12. The postmistress, Marleen, knew everything and everyone. I wondered if she could tell there was something wrong with me whenever I went in. I put on my best mask, my best smile, but taking the Geodon felt glitchy, like I was skipping time. I felt drowsy, light-headed. It currently retails for $154.50 a month.

- Depakote. My cousin takes it, or took it, for migraines. They were horse pills, huge bulbous pink pills that tasted awful on the way down and made me sleep eighteen hours a day; my experience with them was short-lived. $4.

- Lamictal. I took this one for years, at varying doses, and sometimes with lithium or, in time, with one of the many SSRIs or SNRIs I would come to be prescribed. It seemed to help, but also it didn't actually do anything; perhaps I wanted it to do something, so we kept increasing the dose: 100 milligrams, then 150, then more. An anticonvulsant, another one with off-label options. $44.04.

- Zyprexa felt like being underwater. I only ever took it inpatient, and refused to take it when Julie offered it to me on an outpatient basis. I knew what it'd mean: the weight gain, the endless appetite, the way it allegedly changed your blood sugar. Also, it was prohibitive, over $400 a month.

- Risperdal. I took it for years, just a fraction of a tablet at a time. I remember the original package Julie handed to me: warm yellow and pink, with green trim. I remember how she thought it might help. Just a few milligrams at dinner, or maybe bedtime. For sleep, which I wasn't doing enough of at the time. I would cut it up, take fractions of pills, because who could afford it otherwise? $186.93 for thirty tablets.

- Invega made me restless, like the motor inside me wasn't mine. Cash price is $1,289.64 monthly.

- Perphenazine. People used to say Trilafon, because that was the brand name. I loved the idea of taking this: it was an old, second-generation antipsychotic. David Foster Wallace's first published story was "The Planet Trillaphon as It Stands in Relation to the Bad Thing." I found this delightful and it made me less sad, more even, less morose, more socially acceptable, but it also made me chew my tongue to the point where the cashier at Hy-Vee spoke very slowly when I tried to use my card at the checkout. No, I said in a voicemail to Julie's office, after the grocery store. I tried. $64.17 a month on Drugs.com.

- Saphris. Sublingual, like licking a battery. When I went to fill the prescription, it was so new, it wasn't covered under insurance, or there was some trouble with the paperwork, in any case. Julie had given me a blister pack to start, and there we were, suddenly, in the deep end. She wanted me to tell her how I felt about it. It was new. She did this sometimes, presented me with something that had just come on the market the week prior, asked me to tell her what I thought, for her other patients, she said. With insurance, it was only a couple hundred dollars. Retail, it runs $1,263 a month.

- Lexapro. It was supposed to be taken in addition to Lamictal, as a way to bridge the gap between where I was and where I was going to be. If only I could get everything together, figure out how to live, to eat, to take care of myself. $103.77 for thirty tablets.

- Prozac. Three days, maybe four. I stopped sleeping altogether and became angry instead. You can buy it for $166.25 without insurance.

- Effexor was supposed to be an add-on, like Lexapro. I took the extended-release version for a little bit, but it just made everything feel worse somehow. $189 for fifteen extended-release capsules.

- Temazepam. "I'd like to see you four days a week if you're open to it," Lori, my local psychiatrist, said. It was the end of one of our sessions, still early in our relationship; she'd just prescribed the temazepam for the first time. This was one of the medications I took from her instead of Julie. She was different from Julie, from whom I needed a break, more psychodynamic, less interested in the *biological revolution in psychiatry*. If I wasn't at the ER, working with patients or restocking or billing, I was at home, watching things on Netflix. I'd been in my new apartment three months and had just gotten the internet. The drug cost $11, generic. I saw her twice a week at a cost of around $400 a month.

- Inderal (propranolol). Made my blood pressure so low I passed out by the side of the road. I had been driving. Another prescribed by Lori. $152.39.

- Abilify. I started this while taking a class called Nonfiction and the Image, held at a professor's house. I struggled to read maps or hold thoughts in my head for longer than a minute or two. For the class project, I went out into the prairie and mostly photographed dead animals up close. Everyone else in the class found it deeply distressing. I did, too, but I couldn't stop: Deer carcasses made visible from snowmelt. Roadkill. The bones of voles or rabbits from regurgitated owl pellets. The smear of a possum on a shoulder. $904, retail. Even with a prescription discount plan, I remember it being over $150 for the month.

- Ambien. Inpatient only. I'd been told it could be *habit-forming*, so she did not want to prescribe it long-term. $20.48 per pill.

- Klonopin was also inpatient only: nobody wanted you to get hooked. $2.76 per pill.

- Lithium. My most constant. I took the extended-release version, 900 milligrams at night, every night, for years. It cost me the enamel on the backs of my front teeth, my body's ability to regulate its weight, friends, an apartment, years of opportunities, the possibility to drink, the prospect of spontaneity in anything I did, and, ultimately, my thyroid. $19 a month on Drugs.com.

In Telemetry

At my psychiatrist's office, I explained the problem. "I am not sleeping," I said, which was true. I had also stopped showering or dressing appropriately for the weather, but I hoped she did not notice, as I hadn't paid much attention to that either. Everything felt too bright and brittle. My speech was loud and taut—I had too many syllables and not enough breath to say them. I had started seeing her in March the year I was eighteen. By April, I was skipping class to go to the Kalona Sales Barn, where my friend Maggie bought horses out of the kill pen for a few hundred dollars apiece and brought them back to her yard to rehabilitate; I had bought a pony, now named Jack. Just a week into Maggie's backyard equine rehabilitation project, one of them kicked her shoulder and injured her, so periodically I filled in, scooping feed into buckets, hoisting hay over the fence into the paddock behind her house. The sales barn was twenty miles south of Iowa City, and I went there the first Monday of the month to watch Amish farmers trade horses and equipment. In the spring and fall, there was a draft horse and implement sale, which I loved: the way that the horses jangled their harnesses and pulled buggies in the ring to demonstrate their driving skills, the homemade pies and burnt coffee for sale upstairs, women with bonnet strings that dangled over you as they listened in to hear what you wanted to order. The sales barn was where things made sense; you could watch old men run their hands over horses' backs, pick up feet, look at teeth. I wished I were there instead of here.

But in Julie's office, I had failed to conform to the expected

narrative. I was weird, and my weirdness was irrefutable. I studied her quilts on the wall facing me. One was Christmas themed.
She was wearing one of her scarves she had knit herself with
the edges left unbound and strings dangling from either end,
because she had time to make them but not time to finish them
properly. There was a large cup of Diet Coke, from a gas station,
on her desk.

"Emily," Julie said. "I'm on staff at Mercy hospital and it's
an unlocked ward, just so you know." I pretended to examine
one of the quilts instead. The gold thread she'd used to quilt it
curled through the pieced top. The way she had to piece those
triangles first and then press them before seaming them to the
other sections felt studious to me, disciplined, but periodically
you'd find an errant thread, a wobble in the pattern. I thought
about this for a minute.

✧ ✧ ✧

In the hallway outside 4 North, I changed my mind. The hospital
was a block away. I couldn't remember how we'd gotten here.
Had we walked? Teleported?

"C'mon, Em. It's like a nursing home in there. Old people
getting their medications watched because their heart meds
are interfering with all their other drugs. At least come in." We
stood in the stairwell. I had been there before, earlier that year.
She had started me on lithium then. A slow thickness that per-
meated everything I did. The metallic taste in my mouth, the
endless vomiting. All of it seemed terrible and unyielding. I was
not fitting into the world, and so I had been expected to conform in this specific way. Something was wrong; I just couldn't
figure out what it was.

"I—I don't think so," I said. I inventoried myself: charcoal
tank top, green pants, flip-flops—perhaps not the wisest choice

in December, now that I thought about it, *really* thought about it—and my black hooded wool coat that my mother bought for me on sale at Saks. It wasn't really what I wanted, but it was $40. Messenger bag slung over my shoulder: cash, keys, and Mina Loy poems. I blamed one of my professors for suggesting that I look up a Robert Lowell poem. Loy was just beneath him in the library, seductive and incomprehensible. Now I had nothing to read.

At the desk, the woman asked me to stick out my arm. She reached for me with an orange bracelet that said I was allergic to penicillin, and in one swift motion, I withdrew my hand, turned on my heel, and marched toward the door. Turned the knob, pushed, and I was free.

Not crazy, not crazy, not crazy. Fine. I was fine. I had a lab meeting. I had to go to the barn and feed horses. I was not really attending any of my classes. Those people were intimidating, even frightening. I didn't wear the right clothes to class. I knew nothing about Pre-Raphaelite painters. Furthermore, I hated William Morris. *News from Nowhere* was exactly that, Victorian trash, but I couldn't tell anybody, so I slept through slide presentations on wallpaper coloration. In my class on Virginia Woolf, everyone seemed focused on the way she died rather than the way she lived or wrote books. Her diaries were placed on course reserve in the library because everybody kept checking them out. One of the women stood as the voice of mental illness for the class, because, as she confided to us, she had *panic attacks*. When they started showing clips of *The Hours*, I stopped going entirely. I walked back home, lay on my bed, examined the bumps in the ceiling, too numerous to count.

Forty minutes later, Julie called and left a message on my phone. Look, she explained. If it got worse, just come back. What was worse? I wondered. She suggested I take more lithium, just one extra pill, to go from 900 milligrams to 1350. She would write me a script for Risperdal, too, which sounded terrible, but it would help me sleep. Sleep was important, she said.

✧ ✧ ✧

I didn't remember what had started it, a day or so later. I just knew that I had lined up all the lithium I'd had on the counter in the bathroom and it was my responsibility to take all of it. I had locked myself in there and spent some time staring at our tub surround, which was tiled in green and white, a durable ring of mold that bled through both caulk and grout. We had put a table over the soft spot in the kitchen to keep from falling through into the basement, which featured a tributary of the Iowa River. You risked electrocution each time you went to do laundry. It was not a nice apartment.

My roommate didn't know to draw the shower curtain across to let it dry and not grow mold. He smoked. He told lies. He poured salt over everything. We had gotten in an argument again, about what I wasn't entirely sure; I couldn't follow the gist of the discussion. We were not a couple, though admittedly I liked him; he was gay in a somewhat ambiguous, masculine sort of way, and most of my relationships up until that point had been with women. We had met through the improv group on campus, though I never actually joined. He was also shouting at me through the door. Suddenly things felt urgent and strange.

"Open the door or I'm breaking in," he shouted. Was he drinking? Had I been drinking? I didn't think so, but couldn't be sure, or sure why we were there, precisely. I just knew I had to take these, lined up on the counter. I was struggling to fill in what had happened before. I wasn't sure. I couldn't be sure. I filled a glass of water from the tap, and straightened the pills on the side of the sink, which was made of a single piece of cultured marble, beige and plasticky, with sticky, twice-repainted doors and a stained, warped piece of particleboard acting as an inside shelf. There were seventeen pills left; my refill was due a week or so later. Couldn't figure out how I had seventeen; maybe Julie had asked me to take more somewhere along the line? Or I had missed a dose, or three? I normally took 900 milligrams; two pills at 450 milligrams each. So I took all of them instead.

❖ ❖ ❖

Things had not been going well. Everyone else I knew either had their shit together in a serious and satisfying way or else was on disability for their mental illness or perhaps a couple of failed classes away from no longer being eligible for student financial aid. My friends mostly slotted into the latter category, people who seemed to be one or two bounced paychecks from total ruin, people who lived in apartments where the police would follow you home as soon as you turned out of their drive and onto the street. These friends lived in large, brick-and-cinder-block complexes on the edges of town, too close to the Coralville Strip, also known as Highway 6, or else too close to the Procter & Gamble plant on the east edge of Iowa City. My friend Chelsea was in the perpetual student category, with dirty blond hair and a lazy eye that she used for comedic purposes and a 1984 Honda hatchback that finally stopped working altogether, so she abandoned it on the street with the hope that someone would impound it and take it away. Eventually she realized it would make more sense if she junked it, so she did that instead. "Made two hundred and fifty dollars," she explained later, though after parking tickets and fees, it wouldn't cover the costs she had incurred already.

❖ ❖ ❖

There were errors in my chart, but the basic facts remained the same. I remembered coming to for the charcoal lavage, gritty paste in my mouth, the second or third EKG, which showed that my heart had become unstable on account of the lithium over-dose, a wobble in the interval between what I'd learn later was a QT interval and something called T-wave flattening, and that I would have to be monitored until it either resolved itself or I ended up on dialysis. The woman who came around to have me sign for my life, from ER Registration, which would then plunge me into medical debt for nearly ten years, arrived after that. She was officious and brisk, as if suicide was catching, handing me a pen in such a way that we didn't have to touch hands. She wore her brown hair in a long bob with bangs, an ID badge clipped to her hip. Here, she said, and handed me the clipboard. Do you have insurance? I had come here because my psychiatrist had privileges here, at this hospital. Someone must have known this; maybe my roommate had told the EMTs when they arrived to drive my body across town. I had wobbled in and out of consciousness—I remember them arriving, but then suddenly I was in the ambulance, and then I did not awaken again until I was in the hospital, as I was fed the second charcoal lavage. Julie had an office just down the street, this much I knew.

I didn't have a primary care physician or really understand how my insurance policy worked. If something went wrong, I was expected to go to Student Health, on the other side of the Iowa River, in a building I would eventually work in as a student employee for the College of Public Health. I had insurance, technically, but not for mental health care. For my psychiatry appointments—*medication management*—my parents had always paid out of pocket, but recently I'd been running up a bill there, too. The registrar flipped through some additional pages, had me sign in various places. I had been propped up on the bed by a nurse or tech so I wouldn't choke on the charcoal.

The ER felt bright and strange. I had only been to urgent care once before, after a horse fell on me in my teens, and though it was later in the evening, past ten p.m., the place was imbued with busy vibrating energy, the machines beeping and delivering whatever they needed to deliver. My hand glowed beneath two sensors clipped to the end of my index finger. One machine looked like a tape deck and meted out IV drugs (one of the nurses tried to start an IV in one of my hands but had to poke me three or four times); another machine recorded the rhythm of my heart; another still intermittently squeezed my arm with an inflatable cuff, reading out improper fractions: 106/60, 88/56. None of it meant anything to me. I felt woozy and light-headed. The nurses and medical technicians were dressed in different colors, green and pink scrubs, and the doctor flitted between them, spending a few minutes in one room and then a few minutes in another. There weren't a lot of names on the board, but, periodically, another emergency would come in and get set up in a different room, and one of the nurses or techs would scribble something on the big dry-erase board in the middle of the emergency department. It seemed like there was a lot of hurrying up and then hours of waiting; time stretched into the early dawn. There were no windows to the outside, and the resultant effect was that of a ship, warm, snug, coursing through the strange, dark waters of the overnight shift.

✧ ✧ ✧

Upstairs, on telemetry, fifth floor, I had my own room, and the sun cast bars of light across my IV bag and bed. My parents had been called, and were supposedly arriving later that day. It had

taken most of the night to get me here, after they were assured
I didn't need to go to the university hospital for dialysis, and the
early morning sun broke through the windows along the long
side of the room. When it wasn't snowing in Iowa, in winter, I'd
learned, the sun shone oppressively, with low cloud cover and a
persistent glare from sun and newly fallen snow. The IV beeped
and clicked. I was alone.

My health insurance at the time occupied the space between
terrible and nonexistent. There was no mental health coverage,
no way to mitigate what I had done. Nothing quite made sense:
Julie refused to see me in the telemetry ward, so I'd have to
wait until I was stable enough to get transferred to the psychiatry floor. This was frustrating, baffling to me: Why couldn't she
come up one extra floor to see me?

In the meantime, I spent too much time playing with the
plastic shapes that dangled from my IV line, which dripped
potassium and calcium ions in carefully meted doses over the
course of the next two days. Chelsea brought me old copies of
Better Homes and Gardens, rescued for free from some discard bin
at a used bookstore a few blocks away. I split the water-damaged
bits apart with my fingers and examined page after page of gar-
ish geraniums. I couldn't remember if my parents came. We
never discussed it afterward.

"I want to go home," I told her.

"I know," she said, handing me another magazine.

✧ ✧ ✧

They said the word was *noncompliance*, a fancy term for saying
you were sick of the side effects: hand tremors, nausea, weight
gain, sleepiness, or "cognitive dulling," where the mind soft-
ened into some amorphous creature, unfamiliar and familiar
as baby food. The prefrontal cortex, pureed carrots; the cere-

bellum, mashed potatoes. Bit by bit one's brain became dinner. Sit, eat. The nurse told me I was fine. *Medically*, she added. I was lucky, she explained. Without my body kicking in the way it did, flushing the toxins, I would have ended up on dialysis at least, and perhaps on a list for a kidney transplant; also could have had a heart attack, easy. *Oh*, I said.

But I wasn't being discharged.

I was being transferred back to 4 North, the psychiatric wing of the hospital. It took time to sign papers, but eventually I was asked to move; an orderly came in to greet me. He looked like he might be my age, maybe a little older, tall, lanky, pale, some scruff on his chin. He brought a wheelchair, locked it, and immediately bent to unfold the footrests at the base of the chair.

"I can walk," I said. I hadn't yet, not really, except to shuffle back and forth to the bathroom attached to my telemetry room, which was maybe ten steps from the bed. I mostly just leaned on the IV pole I dragged with me. I had felt too woozy to shower, so I hadn't. I knew I looked terrible—I could feel the grease in my hair, the way my face felt heavy and strange, like it wasn't mine. I had looked only briefly in the bathroom mirror. It was not a good sight.

"Hospital policy," he said, and patted the chair. "Sit."

We wheeled in silence: one elevator, then another, then down a long hall to the psychiatric ward, which had a heavy metal door and a small glass-and-wire window. It felt more like a prison than a hospital ward, tucked at one end of the hospital, far away from prying eyes. My belongings had been inventoried and hung in a drawstring bag from the back of the chair. I had been given my pants back; that seemed important. The hospital was too cold to go without them.

On the ward, it looked like it had the first time I'd been

hospitalized: the dayroom, with couches, some tables for where we'd eat breakfast, lunch, dinner, until we were released. A fish tank, with enormous sucker fish that resembled water snakes, their bodies elongated and brought to a dull sheen by the reflection of the tank. End tables. A kitchen (crackers, juice, fruit, milk) on one end, a TV on the other. When people asked me how it was, later, I told them it was great, some dystopian resort.

I checked in, baton passed from telemetry to psychiatry. Here we were. For what, I wasn't sure, still. I did feel better, I kept telling anyone who would listen. I didn't really need to be hospitalized. I was just really tired and took those pills accidentally. I didn't even remember what happened exactly, I said, though this was a lie. I remembered everything, or nearly everything. It wasn't that I had wanted to die, exactly. It was more that I just couldn't keep living.

One room, off the main hallway, was for smokers. "Do you smoke?" the nurse asked me, as she showed me around.

"No," I said.

"*Good*," she said. I looked at her face briefly. I wasn't great at eye contact. It felt like too much, too suddenly. This was why I liked washing dogs at PetSmart or making tables at the statistics lab or scooping sweet feed into a bucket and feeding it to a horse. Faces were strange and unpredictable. Years from now, I would take a test in the *New York Times* that asked you to match the eyes of the person with their emotion. Most people scored somewhere between 28 and 30, or more. I scored 8, mostly by guessing, because all of the eyes looked angry or surprised to me. This woman seemed to have the kind of face that was hard to understand. Her eyes meant something and her body meant something else, but none of it made any sense.

"Okay," I said. There were things I said when I didn't know what to say or how to behave, stuff like "Okay" or "That sounds great; thanks." "Sure!" Or I'd tell a joke. I was good in small, fifteen-minute doses, or less. I didn't know how else to make things work. It felt like there was an instruction manual that everyone else had that I had never received, and it showed up in small interactions, like these, and big ones, like talking to my roommate through our bathroom door. But I could always score 100 percent when I got the mystery shopper at PetSmart, mostly because I knew they always asked the same questions, and I knew the right answers—someone would come to our store, from corporate, to ask us questions about how to shampoo their small dog that got skunked, almost always a Shih Tzu, and to make sure I could direct them to the correct aisle. Nobody's actual Shih Tzu ever got skunked. My aunt had one, and that dog barely left the couch if he could help it.

So I looked at the nurse, who mostly wore street clothes, and didn't even look like a nurse, which I learned later was intentional, *to connect more with the patients*, and I thought of Shih Tzus. She grabbed my wrist and peeled the IV tape off the back of my hand. "This is you," she said, nodding at the door at the end of the hall.

In my room, I curled up in the window ledge and watched the footprints of passersby accumulate on the snowy sidewalks below. I might get a roommate eventually, but for now, the other side of the room remained unoccupied, the thin mattress made up with sheets, one pillow—Lord knows what we'd do with two— and the same kind of lightweight, cotton blanket I had received when I was in telemetry. A woman passed beneath me, crossing the street. A car slowed and she nodded to it, raising her hand, before ducking across the street and onto the sidewalk perpendicular to the hospital. There were a number of streets that just stopped here, briefly, interrupted by the hospital's configuration. She looked normal, probably was, probably on her way to work, or school, or home from one of those. Thinking of daily life felt impossible.

"You know, you'll survive that jump, and it won't be pretty."

I turned. Julie was here. I felt like I needed to practice before she arrived, not to look too eager to see her, to feel like her intrusion was just that—an intrusion. I worried she would see through me, know that I just liked her, that I wanted to see her.

"What?" I said. Had Julie suggested I was thinking about jumping? I was not thinking about jumping.

"I had a patient once, at another hospital, back east. He jumped from the fourth floor and survived. Still depressed when they picked him up off the sidewalk, but now he had a traumatic brain injury, too."

"Oh," I said. "I just want to go home."

My psychiatrist explained that if I left, she'd have me committed, and I'd end up on the other side of the river, locked up at the university hospital with the psychotics. "Your choice," she said. I bared my teeth at her. The depressives, she reminded me, were much easier to work with, in terms of roommate selection. You didn't want to be serious enough to end up over there, on the other side of the river.

"It's not a choice, then," I said.

She smiled. "No, then," she said. "I guess it's not. Why did you do this?" *This* meaning the attempt, I guess, or maybe why I was here at all. Why *was* I here?

I shook my head. "It sounded like a good idea at the time," I said lamely.

I didn't want to be one of *those* patients—too glommy and obnoxious. I knew what those people looked like in real life— entitled women, or girls. *Look at me*, they'd say. They said it in the way they spoke—a raised voice or a lowered one, never a normal tempo or volume; the little rows of scars they lined up on their forearms or inside their thighs; the self-inflicted ciga-rette burns, the disease of starving oneself or throwing up until they became, magically, a certain size. So I had to be careful, to always play back old conversations we'd had, to make sure I was not appearing too dependent or too happy or too sad.

I wanted to be like the woman who crossed the street, who ducked in front of traffic, nodding in the direction of the car that had stopped. She had somewhere to go, was rational, not emotional, smart enough to walk to school without failing to dry her hair. I got lost when I showered—I'd shave just one leg, then forget about the other. I'd walk to places without the right clothes and then realize how freezing it was. Maybe she was a nursing student. That was who I was supposed to be. I was going to be someone, or something, if I could only figure out what that was.

Training Days, or On Experience

We met four nights a week and alternating Saturdays at a partially decommissioned psychiatric hospital on the west side of town. I signed up for the class because I was hoping to get a job working at a hospital or on a rig for an EMS service. I had moved home to the Chicago area because I needed to stop running into my psychiatrist at the grocery store. I needed to get on with my life, I told myself. Get a new job, or maybe an old job, work, make money. I couldn't be the kind of person who ran into my sometime-psychiatrist at Hy-Vee. And, perhaps more pressingly, I'd run out of money to finish the last few classes and owed money to the university, which kept me from re-registering, but I could take out a student loan and take my two remaining English classes at a private college down the street. It couldn't be *that* expensive, I told myself. If I stayed in the area, I'd finish this EMT class, maybe find a job similar to the jobs I had enjoyed most: dog grooming or working in kitchens or maybe something even in medicine.

The class was the EMT-Basic course; prerequisites included a high school diploma or a GED and the fact that you were at least eighteen when you went for your license. If you had the GED, you were expected to pass basic reading, writing, math. We would park in the hospital parking garage and walk down a darkly lit hallway that connected the garage to the hospital; the fluorescent lighting flickered, but the hallways remained dim and quiet. The class, I would quickly discover, was almost all men. There were sixty of them, and six women. The hospital had sixty-seven psychiatric beds, and they were all occupied by people who had cycled through the hospital system, mostly via the ER on the east side of town.

That hospital was known a bit as a knife-and-gun club, the kind of place where you might get complicated gunshot wounds or patients bleeding out in the waiting room. The registration area was protected by bulletproof glass, and you had to be buzzed back to the main ER through a series of locked doors. It was not like the hospital where I'd come to work, but it was useful anyway, busy and full of people in need of medical care. This was part of why I chose this hospital system for my EMS training; I decided I *needed* this, whatever it was.

My teacher's name was Brad. He was bearded and mustached, with a rapidly receding hairline. He'd been a firefighter and fire chief and paramedic for more than ten years a couple of towns over. Less knife-and-gun club, more domestic disturbances, maybe fireworks accidents, car crashes, Jet Skis on the lake in the summertime. It was small enough that they mostly brought their people to the hospital system here, or to another hospital farther south and west. The fire department was across from a strip mall with a RE/MAX office; Three Amigos, which served Tex-Mex alongside four types of queso fundido; Cozy Foot Massage; a dentist; a nail salon. There was not a lot going on out there. He lived around the corner from Hobby Lobby, in a late-nineties two-story builder's spec home, an archetype of suburban sprawl. Three bedrooms, two baths, blue with beige trim, wall-to-wall carpet. I knew because I looked this sort of thing up then. I only did it after he started offering extra credit.

My classmates, as in most of the classes I had taken at community college already, had all sorts of histories. Some of them were eighteen or nineteen or twenty, and some were seventeen and hoping to go straight into the paramedic program. Some of them were thirty-five and had worked in the safety department

at Six Flags Great America for over a decade, and at least half of
them had some kind of military experience or else the desire to
go into the military. When I'd ask around, we had a lot of that
with the younger set, a hope that this certification would be
useful following enlistment, or maybe with a goal to become a
medic when deployed overseas. Some people in our group had
come back from Iraq or Afghanistan, but mostly we were state-
side, hoping to get into the military rather than having already
served.

Immediately after I enrolled in the class, I got a job working at a hospital forty miles away. I got the job because I knew
the doctor in charge of it, a man whose son played hockey
with my baby brother. Sure, it was a nepotism hire, but also,
it turned out, they needed people. Helene, the nursing manager, interviewed me in a tiny room off the main ER, a place
with too many boxes of Kleenex. I discovered later that this was
where they put families after their relative had died. The grief
room, a small vanilla box without windows. My job history was
mostly PetSmart then, some farm work, some copywriting, my
real estate license (it was 2008; nobody was selling their house
unless it was a foreclosure). I'd gotten the license because it
was the family business; it was expected of me. I'd taken a Baird
& Warner real estate class over the course of a week the prior
fall, in a partially dilapidated seventies office building west of
the city. I liked real estate, but at the time there was no way to
make a living; I could barely afford my key fees, much less my
errors and omissions insurance. Helene wanted to make sure I
wouldn't use the phones in the ER to sell real estate. She had
hired someone who did this, once—had a real estate license
and also worked in the ER, like me—and it had gone badly.
"No, ma'am," I said. "I would never." I had worked for years
in college for a statistics lab that ran human subjects. Mostly

Helene was satisfied that I was taking the EMT class, but they would do a lot of on-the-job training once I was hired. I loved the idea of the EMT class, too: it was the place I could go and access some other part of my brain, move bodies, run drills. I liked the physicality of it, how we could touch actual patients, learn to problem-solve in real time, like some medical mystery (it's diabetes, it's always diabetes).

The class was made up of items I remembered faintly from eighth-grade biology and things I felt were common sense. EMS, I quickly discovered, was full of acronyms: knowing your ABCs, or airway-breathing-circulation. We'd do dozens of scenarios with people on the institutional carpeted floor, pretending to be patients. Lying on the floor of a hospital felt unsanitary, but we did it anyway. You'd approach each scenario with hands outstretched, to convey that we were wearing gloves, or *body substance isolation*. "BSI?" we asked. "Scene safe?" Scene safety was the sort of thing that seemed obvious but maybe really wasn't, the way that we were expected to make sure that we weren't creating any additional patients by running in to save the day. This sort of thing happened a lot in stressful scenarios with new and seasoned EMTs; the effect was like wearing blinders, and you'd dive in to save someone from their diabetic emergency only to discover that someone else was brandishing a gun or knife or maybe just didn't realize that you would be helping their loved one and not hurting them. You didn't want to make one patient into two patients or two patients into three. Or there were people with communicable diseases, and despite the expectation that we all had the flesh-eating bacteria MRSA living in our nostrils from working in emergency medicine, it was better if we didn't get sick from our patients. Emergencies are confusing, we'd been told, so it was important to communicate effectively at all times.

Brad was obsessed with the military despite never having

served. He immediately divided our class into battalions, six
people in each: three women in our group, three women in
another group, and the rest, a sea of men, overwhelmingly in
high-and-tight haircuts. Our battalions were supposed to bring
snacks on specified days, do presentations on whatever part of
the body or system we'd been assigned in front of the rest of the
class. It felt suspiciously like middle school, and I hated it. My
battalion included a girl a year younger than me whose primary
role seemed to be to remind all of us of (and educate us on)
her type 1 diabetes. She showed us her pump, how it worked,
its connective tissue, the tiny tubing. She clipped it to the hip
of her jeans and talked about it all the time. "My pump," she
would say. She was into self-advocacy, patients first, being able
to be the expert on your illness. Fighting medicine's patriarchal
institutions. She would stand up for herself, and by extension,
everyone with chronic illness. Her name was Tiffany. Naturally, I
hated her.

'It's hard to explain, now, how I felt then. How I tried to go
to school and go to work and organize my day and remember
to buy groceries and eat them. The class was close to my parents'
house, from which I had recently moved, again, and so most
days I went there to wash their dishes. It was a holdover from
childhood, how my father's interest in democracy meant we
voted on things. "Who votes Emily does the dishes?" he'd say,
and everyone would raise their hands. I wouldn't say that this
was what caused me to be late to class, exactly. It just seemed
like there was always so much to do.

The class kept going. If you were late, Brad would lock the
door, a fire door, a large steel double door that closed with a
lever in the middle and no window, and then make a big deal of
unlocking it to let you in, provided he did it at all. Sometimes I
came to the door and it was locked and I left even though I knew

class was going on inside. I don't think it was a security issue, not really, just a way for him to exert power over us, to make us feel bad and small about being a minute late to class. He emphasized that this was the sort of class that required us to be here every day, on time, no questions asked, no excuses. Otherwise you couldn't get your license at the end of the course—they wouldn't even let you test for it if you'd missed enough classes, though I doubted a minute or two of lateness really counted as an absence in situations like these. One night when I managed to slip in on time, someone brought in the Hare traction to show how it was used, and then we all got to play with it. It was a piece of equipment kept on ambulances almost entirely for motorcycle accidents. The Hare traction was for femur breaks, a way to stabilize the leg and delay shock so the patient could be rushed to surgery on time and without bleeding out. Hare traction, too, was a way to make the pain go away. Femur breaks were supposed to be excruciatingly painful, but it was mostly because the bits of bone dug into the muscle of your thigh. Hare traction kept the top and bottom of your broken femur from touching, made the pain go away, like a magic trick. I both loved and was horrified by the idea of this, that there was so much space in the rig devoted to a device specifically for motorcycle crashes, for when the bike fell on you, and that it worked like nothing else. This was what I felt a lot, maybe, that things kept falling on me.

And then, slowly, suddenly, I stopped being able to make it to class on time, and then, at all. It seemed to meet all the time—Monday and Wednesday nights, each for four hours, or Tuesday and Thursday nights, plus alternating weekends. It was supposed to be the short, intensive semester, the one that would get me licensed before May. My classmates all made it to our class each day. But I couldn't. I would go home to my apartment

for an hour to get something to eat and then fall asleep. Or my
mother would convince me to stay for dinner at their house.
I was falling asleep a lot then. Two lithium pills each evening,
and I had to eat at the same time, to stop from puking. But we
weren't allowed food in class, so I'd have to eat before class, or
late at night, after our class let out. Or at our break, late into the
evening. So at some point I simply stopped going.

And in the meantime, I had patients anyway. At my new job,
one shift, a woman appeared in room 6. In her early thirties,
straight black hair, brown eyes. Rumor was, she was a nurse and
knew how to do it right. I didn't go in there at first. It wasn't that
I was trying to avoid her. More that nothing could be done.
After the initial rush, the tubes, the discussion of what to do. I
had started to do my EMT clinical rotations for Brad's class at
the hospital that was almost entirely trauma patients or complex medical emergencies. Everything felt obvious there. One
patient had a triple A—an abdominal aortic aneurysm—and
bled out internally on the stretcher. Another patient, gunshot
wound, HIV+. Another patient, in labor, no maternity care.
Things seemed grittier and louder there. Here, in the hospital
where I came to work, things felt different. Quieter—though
I learned to never use this word to describe our ER, since our
nurses were superstitious.

Here, there were different sorts of emergencies. There was
less blood on the floor. Yes, we saw kids versus city buses. Or
elderly men who tumbled off sidewalk curbs and into the street
on sunny days. Orthodox women accompanied by six children,
maybe one of whom needed to be seen for a common childhood injury or illness, and the others "just in case." In the case
of this woman, room 6, there was no medical history to take,
no list of medications to scribe, nothing to fetch for Anong, the
nurse in charge of her case. According to her blood draws, and

her parents, she had taken thousands and thousands of milligrams of Tylenol alongside her regular antidepressant. Her liver was shutting down, and they were trying to get her into the ICU, where she would likely not qualify for a transplant. There was discussion about a possible suicide note, but nobody in the ER had seen it. So I brought her a blanket and then another one, shoveling fresh ones into the blanket warmer, pulling the warm ones out, over and over. Rumor was she had drunk alcohol, too, to make it more effective, more permanent. She might die, lying there, and nobody could do anything. I touched her hair. She looked like she was sleeping.

The other techs had taken to whispering, in case someone important showed up. "Bad situation all around," one of the techs said. But I didn't exactly feel sympathy or sadness, as much as I felt I should, or maybe wanted to. More like a slow, quiet envy. Awe, or admiration. Here she was, escaped from this life. She had done what I had tried, and had emerged, victorious, on the other side. Well, almost. For now, we were waiting for her to die. Her parents staggered in and out of her room, exhausted, crying, wordless. They could not explain what had happened to their daughter, and neither could we. I had class, but I simply couldn't go, so I didn't. Instead, I took my lithium and went to bed.

✧ ✧ ✧

Via email, I told Brad that I was sorry I was missing classes, that something else seemed to be going on, that I needed a sort of medical exemption. I was so tired. I had started working second shift at the hospital, and some nights I came home at one a.m. and then slept until six p.m. the following day. Things were not going right for me, for some reason. I tried to be as thorough as I could without disclosing the nature of my illness. I didn't want to be shamed out of this program. Sure, he replied. I could do extra credit, read a book and write about it. He'd send me the information about the book.

I wrote another email to my classmates—my battalion—to apologize for my absence and let them know I'd talked to Brad about my grade in the class, that I would make it up privately. That I had some health issues that had prevented me from coming to class. It wasn't a lie, really, but it seemed like it. It felt like I did this all the time, that my life only allowed for a few things to go right at once, and the rest of the time, I was drowning, or maybe awaiting Hare traction, the splinters of my fractured leg digging deep into the muscle in my thigh. Tiffany tried to tell me how I should be *proud* of my issues, my illnesses. I couldn't confess to them, how my lackluster participation or spotty attendance was in part due to the drugs I took or the feelings I had. *Thanks for your concern*, I wrote. *I appreciate it.* I was so grateful that Brad would let me make up the work with some readings. *Thank you*, I told him. Thank you so much.

✧ ✧ ✧

The extra-credit book was *90 Minutes in Heaven*.

I need you to understand this: I didn't have any exposure to Christianity before. Not like this. My mother was raised Jewish and then became a Buddhist and lately had been attending a Black Baptist church. My dad was raised Catholic and hadn't been to Mass since Vatican II. For a few months in elementary school, when my parents' friends from college moved back from Pakistan and had to wait until their furniture got out of hock— they'd needed to bribe an official to get their belongings out of customs in Karachi—they lived with us, during Ramadan. Every morning at three a.m. we would get up and make pakoras or chutney and we went to the mosque for Eid. I'd attended Catholic schools, at times, but the Catholic schools I'd attended were more lowercase *c*. We had Muslims, Jews. People who needed additional afterschool childcare. Nobody proselytized.

I'm not a Christian, I explained to Brad, in an email.

I think the book still has relevance, Brad replied.

It seemed like too much, this book, the commute to the class. The late nights, the alternating weekends. And the Jesus, which came up periodically in lecture in addition to my extra-credit experience. He started recommending the *Left Behind* books, which I had never seen before. I had to wise up and make sense of what was happening, what this meant. That he wanted to convert us, all of us, sixty men and six women. He was a lay preacher, and we were his flock.

In the weeks that followed, I stopped attending altogether and failed the class, F on my transcript. I had the job at the hospital now, real patients to see. Who really *needed* their EMT certification? Lots of techs in the ER didn't have their EMT because there was so much on-the-job training. I didn't tell anyone; Helene never asked for a copy of my license.

I'd go back for my EMT later, get certified, eventually, National Registry, prove to everyone I could, in Iowa City, hundreds of miles away from Brad and his class. Nobody asked me to read the *Left Behind* novels there. There were no battalions, no group presentations. We just did the work and the clinical exams, extricated each other from smashed-up vehicles behind the fire department training center, cut up cars using the jaws of life.

❖ ❖ ❖

I know I am naive, now. I expect the best in people, that their motives are pure, that they are not trying to convert me or anyone else to their worldview. I don't think that this is an issue for most people. They see what is happening before it happens, or when it happens. I assume everything is fine, that everyone has the same tolerance that I have, if not the same viewpoint. Brad lives in Florida with his family. He has a desk job now and no longer teaches, and I'm grateful. He comes up in conversation sometimes, when I find out that someone's daughter trained at that hospital system, got a dose of Brad's evangelism, his hard recruitment tactics. How it made her feel uncomfortable, how there was a certain kind of patriarchal creep factor in all of it, unnamed but still present. I don't know what to say, so I say yes, me too. Me too.

Three Deaths

He's old. Mideighties, maybe older, in a tracksuit. Running shoes, sneakers, he'd call them, blue tracksuit with white stripes. He is a lifetime of runners in one: the idea of this comes in his legs, sinewy muscle tucked into thighs, adductors, abductors, origins, insertions. A part of me secretly wishes he'll donate his body to a medical school, where he can be admired for months in a cadaver lab, he is so perfect. He's a John Doe so far, which means nobody's missing him yet. I am not sure what to make of this, only he's been in our ER for six hours now, and the thought of being unmissed strikes me as a little sad. He's tanned, his feet proportioned properly, his toenails curled over his toes just a little, as if he was maybe planning on clipping them after he got back from his run later today. Only, the paramedics find him sprawled out on the sidewalk, his legs tangled in midflight.

I remember him this way, later, because he is my first body. My preceptor in the ER today is Ed, a guy who I sell a house to months later, a guy who wants a stainless steel fridge in his condo and makes his wishes known a mere ten days before the closing. We are a little unsure of each other, Ed and I. It is hard to tell when either of us is joking.

"Okay," he says, "this is it. You ever see a dead person before?"

I have: caskets cracked open at Irish wakes, some uncle knocking the side of the coffin with the butt of his beer bottle, everyone dancing. This is different. In his ears there are two earbuds, the music still going in his head.

"Whoa," Ed says, untangling the iPod. "Old guy with an iPod," he says.

Obviously, I think, but say nothing. It's not the iPod that gets me, it's the song, the music, all jumbled in this man's ears while the code pressed on. Nobody claims him, so we page central stocking to come and bring him downstairs.

I normally work second shift, three to eleven or three to one. Three p.m. to one a.m. is best, because then it means you don't get assigned as many shifts unless you want them. The overtime is where it's at. My colleagues and I work like there is no other job, no other responsibility, just here and there, home and the ER. It's hard work, the physical labor of the ER, and an assault on the senses: the work unspools in beeps and blips, clicks and lights. When we get off work, we drink. Glasses of white or red wine, fancy martinis at bougie bars in the stylish part of the city, or else Coronas or Dos Equis, burritos and tacos from places where you have to order *en Español,* or screwdrivers at other bars. It feels like everything is too close, bobbing up against each other, oil floating on the surface in bubbles. We are supposed to work hard, and play hard, and we demonstrate it here, in the work we do, the things we drink, and the cars everyone drives.

Ed is tall, twenty-five years old, and has two cars, a souped-up Honda Accord and a BMW. One of the other techs has a BMW, too. It's funny because we all live at home, or most of us do. I live in a third-floor walk-up, because living at home got to be too stressful, too disorienting, though I'm there every day. At this point, my dad has not left the house in months; my mom works long hours making very little money at all and hangs out with her friends. It is too depressing to stay at home with your father, she keeps telling me.

As a group, we are good at parties: my father, the entertainer; my brother, the musician; my mother, the chef; my youngest brother, our court jester. I function as the dishwasher. But it's day-to-day life that makes for messy living. Nobody knows what we're supposed to be doing.

We need a manual. My mother gets subscriptions to lifestyle magazines like *Real Simple* or *Martha Stewart Living*, but it just makes her nuts: the content isn't specific enough, and the photographs are impossible to replicate. When Martha goes to jail for insider trading, we light candles.

When I was little, my dad started Saturday mornings at six with vacuuming in his underwear, Pavarotti blasting on the record player. Despite having never gone to an actual opera, I know *Carmen* by heart, and it bubbles up when I clean. I come and do their dishes, because without me, they go undone, pile up in the sink, mold and crust, and when people come over, they narrow their eyes at the collection of plates or bowls or pots and pans. Here is the thing: my parents are like children. When I come by, there is no food in the refrigerator. We will inevitably be out of toilet paper, bread, and Jet-Dry.

Once, in college, I extend my stay in Iowa City instead of driving home every weekend like I normally would, and when I finally return, I find my dad standing in his robe and slippers in front of the sink, sipping Raisin Bran and milk out of a glass Pyrex measuring cup. His face is a little wild, unsteady, and he is wearing a week's worth of beard, or more.

"What's going on here?" I ask.

"We are *out of spoons*," he says, and points. And he's right—all the silverware they own is in the sink: a mountain of everyday flatware, good silver, some plastic forks, and some knives I recognize from my apartment, maybe two hundred pieces or more altogether.

"Huh," I say. "I see that." I'm trying to practice my *reflective listening skills*. At that point, I was enrolled in a course for people who need things like *reflective listening skills* to cover for poor impulse control and emotional dysregulation, although my classmates' complaints consist mostly of statements like "the schizophrenic in my group home eats all the good cereal," so I'm not sure I fit there either. When I see the Raisin Bran, the silverware, the beard, I think, yes, the class was worth it. *Be an observer*, I tell myself. This is the kind of thing I am worried about: I can never move away. They might starve to death. Then I think, selfishly: maybe that is not a bad thing.

Ed is hoping to buy a condo or a house, something he can put his name on. He has some money stashed away from when he worked for a trader on the floor of the stock exchange, and he hopes it'll be enough for a down payment. It's 2008, and the market is in the toilet, but where he's buying won't hit real bottom until 2011 or 2012, and nobody knows this, so I tell him he's getting a good deal, that this is a great opportunity, in between drinks at the burrito place one evening after work. There are a lot of us there, most of the techs, all of us second shifters, like Priya, who lives with her mom; Ed, who is looking for a place to live when he goes to podiatry school next year; and some others. I am new, trying out my newly acquired social skills with them, trying to remember what to say and how to act, to behave.

✧ ✧ ✧

The next shift, my dead man is Japanese. When I go into the room, room 13, unlucky for him, I go with the regular morgue kit: body bag, three toe tags, chin strap, chux. The chux is a pad that goes under his bottom, and when Ed talks to me about my job duties as an ER tech, when he talks about the chux, he talks about seepage. *Don't forget the chux.*

I don't.

In the room, I'm alone with the body. This is how you say it: body. Not he, or she, but the body. The family found him unresponsive and called the paramedics.

In the code, there are things you do. Page pharmacy, respiratory, radiology. When you're in the code, you do CPR or run labs to specimen processing, and if there is a save, sometimes a real, honest-to-goodness save, patient intubated, ICU patient, report given, nursing manager paged, the patient's found a bed, the three of us rush to it, me pushing the cart, nurse watching the portable monitor, respiratory bagging the patient—and there is this power in making everyone get off the service elevator.

Today is not that day; instead, we work on this man for his family. Everyone but the family knows he's dead. Paramedics know, nurses know, techs know, just went to bed last night and didn't wake up this morning, seventy-six years old, and that's okay, these things happen.

I scoot him over a little. People say you get lighter when you die, but this is a false statement to anyone who has ever had to untangle a body from all the contraptions of life: Zoll pads for the defibrillator, residue from the leads for the heart monitor. Urine soaks through underpants, maybe a bowel movement. The shirt hangs, cut off.

I push the unzippered bag underneath, rolling him to prop him against the side rail. I place stickers on his three toe tags, slip one over his toe. I wonder if the morticians collect these, like trading cards, some gaudy souvenir. On the sticker, all his identifying information: name, birth date, death date, age, medical record number, his doctor's name, and our ER attending's name. All this, his whole life distilled.

I zip the bag.

Outside, a lone family member waits. Normally the family has left by the time I get time enough to bag the body, but she has been waiting. She is dressed in a business suit, skirt instead of pants, nice makeup, gold post earrings, hose, heels.

"Hello," she says. I notice she is clutching a tissue. When patients come in, they clutch the affected part, as if clutching and moaning will somehow guarantee better service. Family members are about the same.

"Hello," I say. "Can I . . . help you?" What does she want?

"You worked on my father?"

I'm not sure what to say. Normally, yes, I would have. I would have been in there with the EKG machine, running blood to the lab, doing CPR, standing on the little step stool and hammering on his chest. I know what she means, yes, but the answer is no, he died at the end of first shift, and I only work second. Why does she want to know?

"Yes," I say, stupidly. *This is a lie.*

"Thank you."

And now there's no time to say, actually, no, only after he was dead, or oh, that dead guy? I thought you meant the one in room 12, or 11, or 10. But I say nothing. She turns, looks back, smiles at me. Maybe this is it, I have done her a favor, been someone she can thank. Because in death, I am likely spending the most time with him, bagging his body, that any medical professional has spent with him since he came in, including the ride in the ambulance: since we're in an urban setting, the ambulance ride can't have taken any longer than five minutes. The doctor here this morning, maybe Mark, would have called it when it became obvious that the man was already dead. No use wasting interventionist, invasive methods on someone who has no chance of benefiting. I wonder what kind of life this man lives, now dead.

✧ ✧ ✧

We're going to put an abdominal pain in room 14, Ellie, our charge nurse, says. She gives me the evil eye a little because I've already stripped and disinfected a room using the stuff that gives her migraines. It's the only stuff we have, mind you, but Ellie doesn't care; now she can't go into the room to do intake on the new ambulance patient that the paramedics are bringing in in three to five.

"Nicole," she says, so everyone can hear. "Emily did the room with CaviCide, so I can't do intake, will you?" Nicole rolls her eyes. She has been there just as long as Ellie, maybe longer, and is all firecracker and pink scrubs.

"I'll take care of it," she says, taking the clipboard from Ellie.

Where I work, techs do everything. We strip rooms if housekeeping's slow, dip urine for tests, draw blood, and run samples to the lab. We find X-rays on the digital reader and make CDs for patients of their films and stock the urology drawer. We coerce drug addicts to pee in cups and remove the clothes of the mentally ill. We babysit psychotic patients and order meal trays and enter information into the computer and do EKGs and stock the blanket warmer. We operate the bladder scanner, the Bair Hugger, and take rectal temperatures on squirmy infants and elderly people with bedsores. We splint broken bones and push people upstairs onto scarier floors: oncology, telemetry, adult psych, full of floor nurses and unit secretaries who all complain about their single admission. We have thirty-five sick people downstairs and are about to go on bypass, I want to tell them, but I clamp my mouth shut. This is something I am in the process of learning: clamping my mouth shut.

I want to tell Ellie off.

Kathleen, our unit secretary, stands by the door and yells

at us. She smells of cigarettes and sweat and shampoo and has worked here twelve of the last fourteen days, mostly in the same sort of staggery hypnosis, a kind of delirious shorthand we use to try to get by. Everything happens in slow motion: our abdominal pain and vomiting patient is coding in the ambulance bay. The sliding doors whoosh open. One of the cute paramedics (single, I feel compelled to note) is straddling our patient, a fiftysomething-year-old man, both hands clasped one on top of the other, counting chest compressions. They tell you in CPR for Healthcare Providers class that if you're not breaking ribs, you're not doing it right, and the cute paramedic is, his whole weight pressed into the man's chest.

They say that abdominal pain and vomiting is often a sign of a heart attack, but according to the report from the radio just a few minutes ago, they say he's been complaining of abdominal pain for a couple of days, maybe more. No matter: here he is, not breathing, C-mask on, bag valve mask in place, the kind for pushing precise volumes of air into his lungs. The chest compressions are the important part; mechanically starting the heart in atrial fibrillation happens sometimes. There are shockable rhythms, ones that mean you are more likely to live than others. This man has one of those rhythms on the portable monitor. The family is directly behind.

They're heading toward room 2, the room that's best for running codes. There's an adult crash cart already in the room at all times, and like the room's number, there are two of everything: two bag valve masks, two suction canisters, two IV pumps plugged in on poles and ready to go. There are people in room 2, an elderly lady with her daughter and son-in-law, a woman who is fragile enough to be in the big room, who says she's so lucky she's gotten it when I lead her into it and ask her to undress hours earlier.

"Oh, look, Margaret," she says, suddenly enthused. "We got the big room!" If only she knew that we assigned it to her because of her rectal bleed, because she'll likely need two units A negative later on, or maybe because we need a place to set up the CPAP machine for her COPD, or maybe because her pneumonia will mean that respiratory will have to come in soon and provide appropriate breathing treatments; it doesn't matter, not really.

"I need this room," I tell them, unlocking the bed to scoot it outside into one of the hallway spaces that are assigned letters, maybe *H*. I am used to being direct by now, used to telling people things without the requisite *please* or *thank you* normally attributed to these kinds of exchanges outside the hospital.

I do this before anyone has time to complain, because they do, and they will, angry at the thought of being turned out into the hall. This is Ridge Medical Center, they want to tell me. They maybe donated some money to the hospital or else were born here eighty years ago, when it was still called Ridge Valley Hospital—Death Valley for amusement's sake and the history of the hospital's reputation. The thing about being in the hall is that they are unlikely to die today. When I tell patients this, they blanch a little and get quiet real fast. They see the paramedic straddling the patient, the chest compressions, the expressions of the family members trailing behind, and they wise up: this man might die today. Suddenly, inexplicably, they can move into the hall.

Inside the room, one of the nurses pulls Thumper out of the charger. Technically, it's a LUCAS device, brand name Auto-Pulse, an automatic load-distributing band chest-compression device. It straps across the chest and provides compressions in perfect ratios. The Zoll representative has lent it to us for a month to see if our nursing manager wants to keep it and to

see if we save anybody. "Now," he tells us, sliding his hand down
its plastic case, "whichever nurse saves anybody using this baby
gets a fifty-dollar gift card." A chattering erupts from the group
of nurses excited about this news. They've been used in the
field for years, decades, even: rural ambulance services, ones
with miles to travel to the closest hospital, or the flight groups
sometimes use them if they can find a place to put one in the
helicopter. We're checking them out because of our aging nursing population at Ridge, because a lot of the night nurses are
twice as old as the newbies. This is as good a reason as any; plus
there's the gift card at stake.

Proportionally, we save fewer people than other hospitals. I
think about this as we crowd around this man's body so we can
lift him and move him over to a second cart and off the paramedics' stretcher. He smells of sweat and urine and cologne.
We save fewer people because our people are sick and old. This
man is about fifty-five, neither sick nor old. He is younger than
both my parents, who waited too long to have children and
then regretted having them at all. His son is in his late twenties
or early thirties; his son's wife stands next to them, holding the
baby, a boy.

We are all trying to accommodate for the low probability of
saving someone's life. It's some other kind of experience, one
tempered by manual dexterity, of checking twice. Nicole, one of
the nurses, yells out what she's pushing through the paramedic
IV. Ellie yells it back to her and writes it down on the code clipboard. Someone else tries to start a large-bore IV in the other
arm. I shut my eyes and think of the list, the protocol on the
bathroom wall for invasive cardiac catheterization: Two large-
bore IVs, one in each arm, what the paramedics call the coffee
straw because it's the biggest-gauge angiocath you can sink into
someone. A clean EKG. A shockable rhythm. Chest shaved, if

time. The cardiac cath team paged. The EKG machine appears, and I hook it up while Ed does chest compressions on the step stool: we can't get the Thumper working yet, and Ed is already sweating. How many people fit into room 2? Five, eight, ten, eleven.

When I move to Iowa to a big teaching hospital, later, the trauma bays are like theaters, huge rooms for performances, meant for some kind of expert choreography, but instead everyone stumbles at the beck and call of attendings, heat in their voices. People can't find the blanket warmer; they have to be told what to do. At one of these traumas, a boy is ejected from a car outside Waterloo, Iowa, and they fly him in with AirScare, the university's little joke name for the air ambulance service, because of the noise from the helicopters. On the roof the doors slide open and nobody does a hot load, only cold, so they have to turn the helicopter off before pulling anyone out because there is some fear that a tech or a resident or an intern might appear at precisely the wrong moment and lose an arm, a leg, maybe a head, so it's quiet up there on the roof.

In Chicago, at our little ER, this is it: some kind of desperation, this insecurity. Everything goes as planned, but the heat won't go away. It pushes against me, and I see it at once: the man like a manatee, his body slumped back on the cot. One of the attendings is trying to intubate but he can't quite see. His son hasn't left the room, can't stop looking at what we are doing. The daughter-in-law and the wife stand in the hall, the grandson pressed between them. This man is going to die. I push down on the slickened surface of his chest, trying to get the leads for the EKG to stick. I put on the stickers for the five-lead EKG for the monitor. I try to make myself small but useful. My whole life, I have been trying to disappear, hoping for some trapdoor opportunity. Another tech grabs a blanket, a sheet, because there is some worry that someone's actions might be unimportant.

Everything is beeping. I think of the child in trauma bay 2, 246 miles away and six months into the future. His parents don't fit in the helicopter, so they're driving as fast as they can. There is no hand-holding, no thinking of the family here, only chest tubes, the child neatly packaged at the hospital in Waterloo before being transferred. He is fourteen, the same age as my brother, and none of the residents treat him like a human being. He's unconscious, a likely vegetable, a brain bleed, a subdural hematoma run wild, but this doesn't necessarily mean everything.

When we wheel the boy into CT and see the bleed, one of the nurses sighs. Oh well, she says, as if this is it. We take the time to socialize, because he is stable enough to be run through the CT machine without crashing, because we need the CT if he's going to have an emergency craniotomy. The chest tube catches on the end of the CT and I see it and catch it, put the chest tube drainage bag on top of the kid's skinny kid legs: bruised not from this crash, but soccer, maybe. I imagine the clothes he comes in with at the hospital in Waterloo, bagged or disposed of, probably just plain thrown away because of the blood. The downy blond hairs on his calves.

But we are still here, in our little ER, in room 2, the code room. It's my turn for CPR, and Dr. Graham, one of the cardiologists, is already watching the clock. He wants a blood pressure on both arms, but we can't get it on either one. I lean into this half-dead man with my whole weight, one, two, three, four, five, six, seven. I hum "Staying Alive" in my head, because the tempo is right for chest compressions, a little trick we've learned from the paramedics. The Thumper finally kicks into action, but it's not enough. The son watches us, watches me, my hands on his father's chest, hair in my face, his shirt unbuttoned at the collar.

✧ ✧ ✧

In the evening, Ed drives me to his mom's place to pick up some things. The closing's in a few weeks, and we are just finishing up the last odds and ends for his mortgage and making sure that the inspection's clean and ready to go. I am perennially awkward, but there is a part of my life where I can sell a property in two showings. Ed's condo is like this, one bedroom with a den and a nice new kitchen, cheery paint, and light-colored bamboo floors. The sale is a performance, like anything else, and I promise him things I shouldn't, like a new refrigerator, which I end up paying for out of my commission. I'm not sure of the boundaries of our relationship.

His mom is divorced, a travel agent, a profession evaporated with the travel search-engine aggregators, and is never home, he says, as we go inside. It's a split-level, built in the late fifties or early sixties, next to the highway, in a good school district a few minutes from the hospital, and you can hear the expressway from the living room, a low buzz and roar, with all the windows closed. I never meet her but imagine she is the kind of woman who only has one way of moving, and that is forward, into the next thing, and whatever comes after that. You can see it in her handwriting, which peppers the calendar in the kitchen next to the phone in a mixture of English and Korean, the only sign of her presence. The house is small and feels smaller inside, nearly empty of human evidence and devoid of furniture. It feels cold, even though it's a warm spring day outside. He doesn't turn on the lights, and I stand there, in the half dark of closed curtains, as he rummages around to find what he's looking for, checks, I think, for the life he is about to live and the things he is about to buy. Most of the down payment has come from his work as a runner at the Chicago Mercantile Exchange, a job he has done periodically as a favor to someone else, alongside school and his hospital job and everything else. In the hallway, there is the original green wallpaper in places, metallic and ornate, a relic of another time. I watch as he collects the paperwork he needs. In the kitchen, dust motes catch the light of the one window over the sink, and everything feels quiet and airless.

"Listen," he says, and makes eye contact with me. "I don't spend much time here." There is a softness to his voice, a kind of apology, maybe shame. I don't know how to interact with this, what I should do with this news. Yeah, I want to tell him, but I can't claim to understand what it means exactly. I want to tell him that my dad doesn't do the dishes, so he's there but not really there, but that doesn't feel right either. It is at that moment I realize he is offering a space, a place of intimacy, a window into his life, a small door. He has let me in to see where he was raised and why he is buying his own place, which he will decorate, buy furniture for, paint, maybe. Look, he's saying. I'm from here, but look at where I'm going. Look at where I've been. *Here*, he will say, and you will take it, carefully: *Here*, he will say, an offering.

Heartbroke

Angie Day is in love with our EKG machine. She's a tech, newly minted, a convert from the volunteer pool, and this bit of information seems to make her especially dangerous. You see it in her walk: stalking the ring around the nursing station and the doctors' desks, around the Pyxis drawers of medications, angiocaths, IV start kits. The detritus of the day is visible in handfuls: saline flushes in tiny capped syringes litter the counters. Stale doughnuts brought by yesterday's volunteer, a woman who has been here at our hospital since before any of us were born. Angie could sort, or stock, or refill the blanket warmer (the only piece of machinery available to volunteers, so she must be familiar with it). But she doesn't.

Angie's love bubbles up like Bernoulli's principle, increased flow due to increased pressure, a wrinkle in the fabric of the first shift. The EKG machine itself is about as interesting and complex as a dishwasher with a time delay. The EKG doesn't even heat its own hot water. It is, by most accounts, completely worthless compared to everything else: the Bair Hugger, defibrillator, blanket warmer, crash cart, bladder scanner, dental tray, and Thumper, with its exacting chest compressions. Chris, one of the other techs, notices it, too, watches Angie steer it around, both hands clamped to the handles, as if it might roll away without her expert guidance.

Up until now, I've mostly been working with Jim. Jim's my preceptor, engaged to be married despite being only twenty-two, going to medical school in Kansas City in the fall. He is always suggesting I restock the blanket warmer, just in case. He knows things, having worked here for years. "Sure," I say. I am happy to do anything to be useful.

At this point, I have no skills. I know nothing, an empty body, just floating around, some dumb meat puppet, in the way of everyone else. This is who I am now, or maybe it's always been that way. The chronically ill patients, at least the ones who cycle through our ER, are experts on their various diseases. The nurses know how to get their jobs done efficiently and avoid the doctors. The doctors avoid the patients. The other techs, like Jim, have all been here forever. Jim is an expert in the EKG, knows how to draw blood on difficult sticks. All the techs seem to have a kind of specialty. I have the confidence of a sea slug. There is, metaphorically speaking, a line of salt wherever I go. When faced with the physicality of a patient, my body sweats in terror.

Angie is tall and curvy. We don't have any 2X scrubs she can wear, so she wears surgical scrubs instead for her first few days, light blue instead of our normal seal-blue scrubs, and this bit of uniform change makes for a strangeness that's hard to explain. Patients cling to her, presume she's a nurse, tell her the kind of information that normally is conveyed only to the doctor, or at least to a nurse who's been around for a while. I can't even get patients to tell me their names or what drugs they take.

What's more, it's Monday: nursing home dump day. The woman in 6 screams dementedly in Russian; none of our Russian-speaking techs can figure it out. The Haitian woman in 8 wants us to move her purse off the floor because she'll go broke, she is trying to explain. She repeats herself twice to Jim, who only speaks Spanish and English, not French.

"What's that lady saying?" he keeps asking anyone who will listen.

In our hospital, we speak sixty-seven languages. Sixty-seven by the nursing staff and techs and doctors alone. In the ER, we have a language line, in case somebody needs to translate, but nobody ever uses it, and when we initiate new people onto the floor and they ask about it because they've heard we have one from their orientation to the hospital, we can't make it work. It's a computer screen that functions as a two-way video chat, where if we dial a number on the language-line phone, we can get someone who will translate for the patient. The only time I remember anyone trying to use it, the nurse hangs up after twenty seconds of ringing. We don't have that kind of time.

The Haitian woman is speaking French, not Creole, which makes things a little easier. I translate this time, and we move her purse. But nobody seems to be able to communicate with Angie, who cruises the nursing-station ring another time, looking for an acute MI, a prolonged QT interval, even a minor right axis deviation, something.

I am not keen on the EKG machine. I've bought the gold standard book for interpreting the EKGs it produces, a guide by a doctor named Dubin, but I can't be mesmerized by its divine squiggle. All the patients complain about the damn thing. They don't want to sit back flat for the procedure (they have to); they don't want to have the sticky leads placed on their chests, and the women don't want EKG leads beneath their breasts, especially older women, and especially with male techs, who are taught to lift the breast and place the stickers beneath it in a gentle, medically appropriate way. But since our hospital's neighborhood is home to thousands of Muslim or Orthodox women, the female techs end up doing most of the tests.

Angie and I see more electrocardiograms than the male techs. It is only a fraction of our job, but an important one nonetheless. If the EKG has too much squiggle, the docs make us do them again, because they're impossible to read. I know what a normal one looks like, sure, but for the rest you rely on a printout of the information on the top of the EKG itself. Later, the data sends itself upstairs to the cardiologists, in case there's something the docs miss down here. I have only had to redo two EKGs since coming here, one for a pregnant woman who refused to lie on her back, so the result looked like a sine wave. The other for a man with Parkinson's. I know the drill by now: tell them it won't hurt, that it'll just take a few minutes, that we just need you to lie down for a minute of it, that the most important thing is to relax as much as possible and breathe regularly, in and out. Think of nothing, I tell them.

Of course, nobody actually needs one right now. Here is the board for today: three nursing home dumps, one "fall down go boom" (EKG done already, and besides he has a pacemaker, so it's not going to change anytime soon [we hope not, anyway]), man versus meat slicer at work, kid on bike versus city bus. We say "fall down go boom" for patients who do exactly that, mostly stuff that results in a loss of consciousness, a heart thing or an overactive vagus nerve or something else entirely. It's odd, because we normally spend tons of time working with the EKG; both machines (we have two) are constantly in use throughout the day, every day. We have plenty of sick people.

I have this job because there is PTO and maybe benefits if I stay. I'm making $11.35 an hour, day shift, because I'm new and I haven't been fully trained or gotten the shift differential. This job is better than making $9 an hour as a paramedic on a rig in the city. I thought about going to paramedic school, but I can't even think of how it'd make sense to make $9 an hour when I get out. I have no idea what I'm supposed to do with my life; I never anticipated living this long, so I'm just here, faking it until I figure it out.

"Why don't you plug the EKG back in?" I say, tentatively.

Angie just glares at me. It's her first real hospital job, a first opportunity to be a certified medical assistant, a way to get health insurance and bennies and paid time off. The PTO is really a great draw. I use it to pay my car insurance periodically. Most of the techs use it to pay for their college tuition. They'll be doctors someday, all of them: Jim to the osteopathy school in Kansas City, Ed and Amanda to podiatry school, Ekaterina at Northwestern. But Angie's in it for the long haul, she says. This is her lucky break, her life measured by dental insurance and free parking at the hospital. This is what it's like for day-shift techs. Second shift or third, and it's all students, young people, EMTs, maybe future doctors or pharmacists or something else. We are all on our way to somewhere else. But the day shift are lifers, women in their thirties or forties or fifties who can get off work at three p.m. and go pick up their kids. Angie's kid's maybe four now, with a button nose and a big grin; his picture's on her cell phone. She says she's doing this for him, which makes it sound sweet, but really she spends hours on that phone during her shift, yelling at her mother who is apparently not able to take appropriate care of her son. Our hospital does not offer childcare of any kind.

✧ ✧ ✧

It's the beginning of third shift, close to the end of my day, almost one a.m., when we realize. Or rather, I don't. Rich, one of the docs, is the one who notices the discrepancy. Rich is the kind of guy who was a paramedic first, which means I like him. Also, he lets me glue people's foreheads together with Derma-bond by myself. This is another very good reason to like him. He has a kind of part cavalier, part disaster management approach to the practice of medicine. I bring him an EKG from a guy with a history of acute MIs, a guy who throws PVCs, or *premature ventricular contractions* for the uninitiated. They're like hiccups of the heart, a small lump in the EKG's quaver, a skipped beat, a flutter in the chest. Patients can feel them sometimes, feel like they've missed out on the *dub* of *lub-dub* regularity, and this makes them potentially harmful, even dangerous. The heart is a pump, a mass of electrical signals hopping from one side to another via nodes, and the PVC is like somebody's jumped rank, because the heart's ventricles are stimulating the contraction, not the node that's supposed to trigger it. Our guy in 12 knows what this means for him, probably an overnight stay. We've already seen one too many skip across the screen on his monitor. The EKG is just for paperwork's sake.

But the EKG is wrong. It says there's something else wrong with him instead, not just a PVC, but a different kind of scribble, one opposite what we expect: an ST elevation, which, sure, is associated with heart attacks sometimes, maybe even often, but not in this guy. The EKG doesn't match the output on the monitor, not by a long shot, and when I bring the readout to Rich, he frowns.

"This isn't right," he says.

I bite my lip, start formulating the right words: *I'm sorry, I'll do it again, Doctor.*

But before I can speak, he shakes his head. "This isn't right," he says, again. "I've admitted two people with this same EKG already today. This *same EKG.*"

Now it's my turn to frown. Rich is not the best doctor. He's the one who orders too many tests and blood cultures on everybody who might have an infection, which is nearly everybody who comes into the hospital.

"What do you mean?"

"This same EKG," he repeats. He's beginning to look a little crazy. "Can we look and print off the old EKGs from earlier today?"

We can, and we do; and he's right, they're the same. Two, now three EKGs, all identical, all for different patients.

"I admitted two people today to telemetry beds based on these EKGs," he says.

I make a sign that says, PLEASE DO NOT USE THIS EKG MACHINE ☺ and clock out.

✧ ✧ ✧

In the morning, I get a call from our nursing manager, Helene. There's an inquest of sorts, a conference, trying to find out what happened to the machine. Someone from HR has come down to interview everybody. Apparently someone has switched the arm and leg leads, and this is why it hasn't worked. Angie and I are the only techs who used the machine before it got screwed up, and after. These are facts. It's like a kind of stochastic process: it could be either of us, but some events are more likely than others, which is to say, Angie switched the leads.

The next day a woman comes to watch me use the machine. I go through how I've used it and the steps I complete in order to make everything happen. In my head, I pretend I'm running a QVC channel, so I do a lot of demonstrating with my hands. "Here, I make sure all the leads are firmly connected," I say, as I pick up the giant plug to which all the leads are connected. On the other ends are colored clips that tell you where to clip on the stickers you put on the patient's body. "When I was trained," I explain, "I was told to make sure all of the leads were connected before I pick up the receiver."

The HR woman nods. The woman—she said she was from HR, but later I'd understand she was performing a bit of an M&M conference (morbidity and mortality, though nobody had yet died)—says, "Show me."

It seems silly. Was there another way to do this? I wondered. Was I doing this correctly? I pick up the cartridge and demonstrate how I'd apply the leads to the patient. "I make sure everything is firmly connected again and ask the patient to lie still while the EKG is performed." This had not always been the case, as I had patients who refused to lie still, preferring instead to fidget, forcing the EKG to be repeated five minutes later. When showing it to a doc, they might say, "Um, is this a patient with Parkinson's?" and if I said no, I'd have to do it again, reemphasizing to the patient that no, it was not an MRI or a CT scan, but it was still vitally important that they be still during the procedure.

The HR lady turns and looks at me when I am done. "Anything else?"

This sounds like a trick question. "No," I say. "But when I'm not using it, we try to leave it plugged in, in case of emergency. When you have to use it for continuous EKG monitoring, it drains the battery pretty quickly."

She nods, her sandy blond bangs bouncing in front of her eyes, then puts her hand on my shoulder, though I am taller than she is. This is when I realize she is not from HR. "Thank you, Emily. You've been very helpful." She is satisfied with my explanation. She has decided it's not me.

This had been a kind of risk assessment, a way to determine who was at fault and where our training had gone wrong. I didn't know it then, but I had passed.

But that means it's Angie.

✧ ✧ ✧

Angie appears the next morning, same as usual, first shift of
the day. She frowns at me, at the empty blanket warmer that
needs to be refilled, at the man in 17 who fell off a ladder with
a circular saw and gutted his thigh like a fish. The EKG has
been "fixed," the leads switched back, the order of the universe
returned to a normal chaos. It's Friday, which is busy for us.
I watch Angie as she unplugs the EKG from its charger and
lopes around the nursing station again. Helene calls her into
her office, the EKG machine left in the hallway between beds
J and K. I plug it back in. I don't want the charger to die if there
is some kind of regular emergency. It should be kept plugged in
for especially this reason. In just a couple minutes, it's all over:
Angie, stomping across the slick floor, out of Helene's office,
past the nurses' station, phone in her hand.

✧ ✧ ✧

I'll merely wonder how many patients were admitted (Three?
Four? Two? Each number seems like too many, though I was
never told) under the guise of a long QT interval or an ST elevation. Or, worse, how many we failed to admit because the
EKG was incorrect and told them they were normal when they
weren't. It'll be okay, I'll tell myself, because they alerted anyone who received an EKG from the faulty machine. There was
a way to document this when the data was sent upstairs to cardi-
ology. Innocent mistake. Anyone could have done it. But it's the
fact that we did—and we did without looking, without thinking,
that makes this case resurface again and again. In patient care,
there are only so many mistakes we can make before something
truly terrible happens. And then, what then?

✧ ✧ ✧

In an alternate universe, I confess to the crime. I let the charger disconnect from the metal wire leads and put them back in a haphazard way, thus causing the errors in the EKG. I dream about this possibility: what if, what if. I walk through the steps again, making sure that the EKG is secured. Leg leads and arm leads and ventricular leads, all of them. There are twelve of them but only four or five colors on most models, as arms and legs are pairs, and thus coded the same color. I think of the clips at the ends of the leads, how each of them spelled out where they needed to go. LL for left leg, RA for right arm. The one that went right over the heart, coded red, and the other one that went next to it. V1 through V6, the ventricular leads scattered across the chest and around the rib cage, curling around the base of the heart like a strange, wiry embrace. I think of how I would press into patients' skin to count ribs to make sure I placed the leads correctly. It was an older machine, so you had to pull the holder for the leads out first, a two-handed operation. I'd grab the charger with my left, the wires with my right, and lay them across the patient.

✧ ✧ ✧

I don't know who's supposed to pay for it. How we are supposed to do anything, now, to figure out who gets blamed. How to behave. What to do after all these people were admitted to telemetry beds. Ultimately, the hospital pays, we're told, but it's not that simple. There are these conferences, I know, M&Ms, morbidity and mortality. Conferences where people speak internally about what has happened so they can avoid doing it again. Years from here and now, I will work for a physician staffing agency on their medical education program and run one of these internal panels for the company. We are supposed to learn things from these sorts of conversations, but all the physicians from the staffing agency are afraid to submit cases because they don't want to get fired. So I make composites, like this case, used as an example of what not to do, how to not do this again. Because, I tell the group, it's maybe not exactly Angie's fault, but maybe it's Helene's, or Rich's, or Jim's. Maybe it's mine. Or maybe we need universal childcare, too, though I don't say this. I don't know if Angie is fired or if she quits, but the result is the same: I never see her again.

Soft Restraints

The woman blew in on a Thursday, early into second shift. It was late spring. Things had begun to heat up outside and in the ER, a kind of June panic that meant admissions increased as the temperature rose. Spring fever, the nurses called it. I had been working in the ER for a few months by now, where patients flowed through the premises with some degree of repetition and regularity. These were patients who saw us as a kind of checkpoint between here and there, a middle ground. One of the hospitals in the area was great for having a baby. Another had a helipad and seemed to get all the trauma cases. We were the ones with the locked psychiatric ward.

She seemed less a person and more a force, in her late twenties, light brown hair, blue eyes, medium build, and, when I first saw her, thrashing up and out of the bed, as if in seizure. By then, I had some experience dealing with patients, and she seemed no different at first, just louder and harder to understand. When you see someone on the worst day of their life, it is hard to know what to say or do, but you learn, because there are so many of them and they are all having the worst days of their lives. In a sense, most of the ER was about worst days. If they felt better, they would be at their own physician's office, or at home, or buying bags of frozen peas in the grocery store. This was a woman I could see buying frozen peas. I thought of her pink, manicured hand dropping the bag into her cart. Maybe her name was Elizabeth.

Elizabeth thrashed and cursed. "Don't touch me!" she screamed at our charge nurse, Ellie, who was trying to start an IV. The ER was laid out in an oval, with a ring of rooms on its perimeter, and the nursing station and the doctors' desks inside. Katya, the other ER tech, and I stood at the edge of the ring, leaning up against the counter that separated the station from the hallway, directly across from room 14. Elizabeth kept kicking and screaming. She wasn't sorry, she didn't care what our charge nurse had to say. She would not submit to a tox screen, thank you very much. And she was disinterested in voluntarily participating in whatever we had on offer, which in this case involved restraints. So she kicked and screamed some more, while Katya and I watched from the hallway. Katya was practical, even-tempered, career-minded. She was going to go to medical school eventually, once she retook the MCAT and scored well enough to get in. She had been a tech for years; working as one created an important but temporary space between childhood and the rest of her life. She had lots of experience working with lots of patients, and had also worked at hospitals much scarier than ours. "I don't want to go in there," Katya said, a little under her breath.

I had reached this part of my life unexpectedly, hadn't anticipated ever becoming an adult, and yet somehow I was, legally, of age and expected to get along in the world. I had some vague idea of becoming a doctor, too, but that was hard to explain to others at twenty-two when they found out I had half an English degree and none of the premed requirements completed except as audits or withdrawals on my transcripts. I had tried to enroll in chemistry or biology, but the work of those classes was far beyond the reach of my abilities. The classes were huge amphitheaters of teaching, and if you were late there were not enough seats and so you'd have to sit in the hall, which compounded my problem. I tried taking a class at the community college but that too moved too quickly and without the necessary pauses so I could understand what was being said. The labs were full of people who seemed to know intuitively what to do, how to pour the alcohols, to light the Bunsen burner without incident. A flick of the wrist here, some neatly copied equations there, in graph-paper notebooks. I kept taking these classes even though I had no hope of passing. It was like this: I liked to pretend I could do it. And becoming an EMT still felt possible, made me feel closer to bodies, science. Being an EMT, or at least an ER tech, offered me a kind of legitimacy.

In emergency situations, there are two types of restraints: hard and soft. Hard restraints are the stuff of television, the story of the patient sitting up and biting or striking a resident with an open mouth or a closed fist. It's the part of the show where the attending swears at a patient. They're locked with a key affixed with a magnet to the Pyxis at the nursing station. What most people don't realize is that it's soft restraints—white, padded, and Velcroed—that are used most frequently, mostly for patients who are at risk of something happening to them. These are the patients who injure themselves by crawling out of bed, or falling, or perhaps they have end-stage dementia and they can't help but pull out their IV to spray blood around the room and spatter the privacy curtain drawn between patients. Patients who fiddle with bandages, or who scratch where they shouldn't, get soft restraints. For nearly everyone, we give them the benefit of the doubt: usually we start with soft restraints and move to hard should the situation warrant. There are rules. With Elizabeth, it seemed we would have to immediately up our game.

There had been other patients before Elizabeth that day. I worked mostly on the fast-track side of the emergency department, saw kids with kids, orthopedic injuries, new mothers who needed reassurance that the pediatric Tylenol was correctly dosed, men who had removed fingers in meat slicers, toddlers who had faced brick walls or concrete sidewalks and lost, split open a forehead or scalp and needed sutures or staples to put everything back together again. Earlier in our shift, a Muslim woman came in with a rash on her face that might have been lupus. It was never lupus, and yet there it was, butterfly stretched across her face, the top of each wing swooping to touch her hijab. Once we stopped laughing in the hallway at how strange it was, our gallows humor, like from an episode of *House*, someone went in and informed the patient, who was told to see her primary care physician immediately, and if she didn't have one, that we'd find her one. She insisted that I stay with her whenever our PA, who was male, examined her, and wasn't comfortable with a full exam in any case, so I was the one who took her temperature and blood pressure and touched her. I wanted to feel awful for laughing, but none of us did, not really. We laughed because people kept dying, and if you were not having a heart attack or a stroke or maybe had a broken arm or needed sutures, we typically did not know what to do with you. The lupus was so easy—*for once*, a relief, a diagnosis smacking us in the face. But by then, midway through the afternoon, the woman with lupus had been discharged, and so we waited for the next drama to slide through our doors.

I occupied the world of the physically well then, or I thought I did. I had not yet been told my thyroid had stopped working, or that the lithium I was taking had likely hastened its demise. That would come a year later. There was no autoimmune asthma diagnosis then, no concerning liver results, no vomiting every time I got my period, no inflammation markers in my labs, no pain in the mornings that radiated from my joints and muscles and ran down my arms or legs.

✧ ✧ ✧

Elizabeth wasn't assigned to me, but I knew her from before, from prior worst days. She was what we called a frequent flier, someone who was unable to make sense of the world she lived in and so she came to us instead, a kind of tent revival in our sub-urban hospital, for healing. She had been previously diagnosed with borderline personality disorder and fibromyalgia and had a history of drug dependence. And some sort of digestive ail-ment, because everything was and is related to the gut, though few people treated patients with this in mind. Mark, the physi-cian assigned to her, was not one of these types of practitioners. The fact that Elizabeth had fibromyalgia alone meant nobody in the ER was about to take her seriously. It was a made-up diag-nosis for us then, a kind of early aughts placeholder for female hysteria.

I, too, had a problem with being taken seriously. Not here, exactly; here I showed up for my shifts on time, learned the give-and-take of conversation, how to address patients, heard their stories, wrote down what drugs they took, performed EKGs, and drew blood. And my job was time limited: the cost of doing business never lasted longer than a shift. But I was odd; I had difficulty understanding when I should speak and how far away to stand from someone else. When I interviewed for this job, or any job, it was a kind of performance. I made great first impressions, but for those who got to know me, I might let my mask slip, and could be intense in a way that some found off-putting. Here was another strangeness: I flapped my hands when excited or nervous or sometimes out of frustration, but mostly I did not know where to put myself. In a strange way I believed I understood how Elizabeth's tragedy unfolded day after day. The night I showed up at Mercy hospital, Iowa City, how I barely remembered the nurse who cared for me, the tech, how the pair forced my arm away from my mouth and administered two charcoal lavages. I remembered the second one: I was conscious then. For them it was another shift, this lifesaving work, and for me it was the last day of something and the first day of something else.

Elizabeth stopped for a minute and looked up at Ellie, the charge nurse, who was speaking to her. I had turned away by then; I had other things to do, drawers to stock, patients' drug lists to inventory. The man in 6 had just brought in an Altoids tin full of pills and had dumped it on the side table, and I had been tasked with finding out what all those drugs were and what he was taking them for.

But Elizabeth in bed 14 wouldn't stop thrashing. This was an act, it seemed. Everything sublimated to the performance. We had been drafted as Elizabeth's audience, and we were here for something stark and unimaginable, something important and fierce. The charge nurse was there to bear witness, or maybe the patient was possessed. Years from now I will glamorize this situation, this moment. Maybe she is blond after all, or maybe she is wearing makeup, or not. I can't say now. It's hard to know for sure. I want her to know that we all saw her. I was tempted to touch her, to see if she was, in fact, real, but the charge nurse wouldn't let me in, not after what happened. "She's not your patient," Ellie said, which was fine in some ways and felt untrue in others. She might be my patient, I thought. She might be me.

✧ ✧ ✧

In the X-ray alcove off the main ER, I pulled up films of a woman whose head had grown an orange. It was like that, some days. You could find people whose systems had gone completely, wildly awry. The woman had a headache for a week, the worst headache of her life, and once we put her through the CT machine, we saw it, a white ball, a little more than five centimeters across, roughly the same size as the small oranges you could get for seventy-five cents each by the checkout lady in the cafeteria. I found this news thrilling, devastating. How our bodies betrayed us. Someone, definitely not me, probably Mark or the other doc staffed that afternoon, would have to tell her. She was in room 12 and would not stop crying. I think this was part of the brain tumor, too, though in truth I had no idea. We had not discussed brain tumors in my EMT class. Mark came in and looked at it. Mark had a practical approach for the practice of medicine. He had problems with patients whose problems could not be immediately solved in the ER.

"Wow," he said, tracing the orange with his index finger.

"Yeah," I said. When she came in, everyone had assumed she seemed a little wild, panicky, maybe floridly psychotic. Usually things like this were some kind of conversion disorder, or maybe psychosis. She was categorized in some ways like Elizabeth had been. But the crying felt weird. The headache felt weird. So off she went for a CT. We usually waited for results from the radiologist before taking a look ourselves. Not today: the answer was obvious.

"I thought she had gone off her lithium," he said, staring at the orange.

"I am on lithium," I said. It just slipped out.

He turned to look at me. It was dim inside the X-ray alcove so we could read films more easily; the side of his face glowed from the screen of the reader. It felt difficult, suddenly, to make eye contact.

"Did you eat lunch?" he asked.

"What?"

"Lunch. You're supposed to eat lunch. To metabolize the lithium, especially if you're doing something like working second shift. Are you okay?"

He looked at me with something like earnestness, or maybe pity. I don't know why I said anything. I never said anything. I had said precisely nothing to any of my other coworkers; sometimes when we went out to drink after work I'd skip that dose just to be on the safe side, since lithium and alcohol weren't supposed to mix. Here, in the ER, I was someone who had learned a certain level of competency. Not respect—respect was not it. But competency, sure. I could fetch things and get things and pull films up on the X-ray reader. Now all that seemed to evaporate.

"I'm fine," I said. "I'm careful." I was under the care of a very good psychiatrist in Iowa City, I explained. I drove to see her once a month or so. But even this idea, that Julie was very good, felt more and more untrue as time went on.

"You have to be careful," he said, studying me. Me as competent tech had simply evaporated. Here I was, a possible patient.

I knew I had said the wrong thing.

But this sort of situation—where we treated medical patients as if they had psychiatric complaints—happened all the time. It had happened to me, to Elizabeth, to this woman with an orange in her head.

"I'm fine," I repeated.

She had had "the worst headache" of her life, she'd said, and just for fun, we'd put her through the CT machine. It probably wouldn't yield anything, we told ourselves. They say that now CT scans account for half of the radiation exposure for American patients like this woman, up from about 15 percent in 1980. It is so much easier to look for the problem with a picture than relying on medical deductive reasoning or stethoscope skills, so this is what happened. It probably wouldn't tell us anything, we were told. But then it did: a tumor, 5.2 centimeters across, a bright white ball the size of an orange. There had been signs; she'd been forgetting words, she explained.

✧ ✧ ✧

Mark didn't think I was weird forever. Maybe I imagined the way our relationship changed. Maybe it didn't change at all. Mostly I worked in the Fast Track side of the ER, got competent at splinting broken hands and radii and ulnas, so I didn't see him much. When our paths crossed, his gaze didn't linger.

My problems looked like Elizabeth's, stretched far beyond my ability to manage the day-to-day work of living: I had sleep disturbances, failed to make appropriate friendships, lived in a well of loneliness of my own making, routinely fantasized about killing myself, and perhaps strangest of all, had a woman in my head who narrated everything as it happened, someone whose apparent role it was to be a kind of judgy commentator, a lens through which I saw the world. She was certainly not me but helped me practice what to say before saying it; in any event, I had little control over what she said. Later, I realized she was telling me what to write down, and that I didn't have a mental illness after all, but for a while, this was a hard thing to explain to my psychiatrist, who saw the world in narrow, rigid categories, as if sanity were a tightrope stretched between here and there.

✧ ✧ ✧

When I see Elizabeth's face, or the orange woman's expression, in our ER, I think of her, of me, time spent in emergency situations, and I wonder how wide my own path is, balanced on the thin edge of a knife. I don't want to be Elizabeth, but I feel like I could have been her, some kind of shadow life, some alternate reality where I didn't opt out of that sort of psychiatry and into a good therapist, one where I kept seeing Julie or some other psychiatrist whose sensibility about medication and management looked about the same. Somewhere where I didn't get diagnosed with thyroid disease or started eating differently or addressed my vitamin deficiency or got away from beneath the thumb of my own upbringing.

✧ ✧ ✧

I know the things I experience are real. I also know that it doesn't take much to get addicted to someone taking an interest in who you are, that sometimes all you are looking for is an answer, an explanation for why you feel this way, maybe a box to check or a space to occupy. Validation is vital. I took twenty-six medications because I wanted to believe in the psychiatric medical establishment and trust the woman who cared for me, who I believe was doing the best she could with the resources she had. I was still unwell, and perhaps there would be a drug to fix me, if only she could find it yet. I still want to believe, though I carry a different diagnosis now. The way in which you think that things are supposed to work, they hardly ever do, and yet.

✧ ✧ ✧

Now, a decade later, I live in a neighborhood two blocks from a group home and rehabilitation center. The rehab part is mostly a lie, as patients are churned through. They come in for a medication stabilization and then slip out the door again to places unknown. The company that runs the home calls it an intermediate care facility, which is what patients call "residential" after they've been transferred from an inpatient facility in a hospital, like the one where I once worked. This is the holding area, the place to house 417 people who have nowhere else to go. Probably a relative of theirs fought to have them hospitalized here instead of somewhere else farther away or with poorer reviews. They congregate in groups in the park across the street from the building where children never play, and smoke and talk to themselves and each other to pass the time. The residential care facility is something of a liability in our neighborhood. It means that there is a large man, a longtime resident, who wanders our streets, accusing passersby of stealing or starting fires. There is a thin, elderly woman, who is probably less elderly and less frail than someone might think, who paces our neighborhood with a walker in a dirty windbreaker; an emaciated guy who panhandles for fifty cents at a time outside the fabric store; middle-aged, soft-looking women in grimy pajama bottoms and T-shirts who address you in a way that reveals a kind of intimacy wholly inappropriate for strangers.

There is a red light near the facility that stacks cars eight or ten deep, so that you can't help but pull up alongside their door. This is part of my commute now, right on Ridge, left on Crain Street, around the bend, and then left on Dempster and out to the highway to this job in my future life. When I idle the car in traffic, this feels like another choice, a pull, albeit one I did not make. I sit in the adult car I bought after accepting a new job. It is nice and I spend a lot of time in it now, commuting back and forth to my new job, this other space where I exist in a mostly analog format. I smile and talk to people, remember coworkers' birthdays, keep fidget toys or candy at my desk to show that I am inviting, friendly, playful. I am careful to regulate what I say, how I say it, who I am, who I appear to be. I pass, more or less. I brush my hair and teeth, wear clothes that signify that I am performing office life. But this is not an easy choice. It is, however, a choice, at least for me, at least for now. It is a choice I make every day.

✧ ✧ ✧

In truth I live two lives. In one, it's here where I live with my husband and our dog, the latter of whom is dying of cancer and has not informed us of this fact, so we walk the neighborhood like everything should be sniffed but ultimately is fine. We bought this three-flat with my husband's savings and a student loan I took out shortly before graduating from graduate school and floated all our renovations with my salary as a medical writer and project manager for a pharmaceutical company eighteen miles away. There, I worked on drugs that affected the central nervous system. I used the same shorthand I use for all the jobs I do in this industry: *I know about that drug, oh, used to work on an ad campaign for that antidepressant or this antipsychotic,* and maybe that is what gets me through, a kind of confidence and bluster, a familiarity. But I also have personal experience with the twenty-six medications I was prescribed and then discontinued between the ages of eighteen and twenty-four. I think of that time I told Mark, and then I think of nothing. What could I even say to my coworkers now? This is still too much to tell.

But still I pass the group home in my neighborhood on a regular basis. I scan the crowd, looking for Elizabeth or someone who approximates her. I told our friends I picked this neighborhood because it is the only place where it is okay to talk to yourself on the street. I feel at home in a way, but proximity to the residential center makes me wary, like it's a hole I could slip down if I get too close. So I cross the street when I pass it by, or speed up a bit in the car, try to adjust my hair, my clothes in the rearview mirror, blot my lipstick, make sure it's still me, and drive away.

For Pain

The pain began with a traffic accident. Kathleen was seventeen then, rear-ended, not her fault, just idling at the wrong red light at an intersection two miles from home in Des Plaines, Illinois. It was dark, maybe raining, and the impact pushed her car into the intersection like a shuffleboard puck. The pain arrived almost immediately after that, spread across her back, down her legs, into her shoulders and upper arms, which ignited with pain. In the body, there are dermatomes, maps for ways in which pain travels, and her pain lit up areas nine and twelve. She had been hit in two places on account of the crash and injured both cervical and lumbar vertebrae. The other driver did not have insurance.

The spinal nerves did the work of carrying the pain to new places on the map, underneath and outside her body, up and down the legs, baton passed like runners in a relay, the heat searing beneath her skin, down to muscles and joints, sinew of ligaments and tendons, bone thrumming underneath each step.

The pain, like anything else, was not constant, but close: it chased the edge, lapped at the shore. She started to get migraines. She lost her job working the ambulance service as an EMT because of the physical demands and the grueling shifts and got a job manning the front desk at the hospital where I came to work. She did clinical intakes, told the paramedics where to send bodies, alive or dead, broke down charts, and ran the front desk of the ER when needed. She ordered supplies and directed traffic and helped make the schedule for us techs.

Sometimes she worked as a tech, too, if we were short; Kathleen still had her EMT license and her medical assisting certificate earned from a for-profit college down the street. She stocked drawers and assigned IV pumps to rooms, made them stop beeping when the cartridges ran out, flirted with the paramedics, called for maintenance on the EKG machine and the bladder scanner, could troubleshoot the blanket warmer if needed, or run blood to the lab when the pneumatic tube system was slow or out of service. In the ER, machines and people were her domain, and she ruled all of it from a perch at the front desk with the other unit secretary, Myla, who worked alongside her.

Her physician, the man who came to manage her pain, practiced out of the office building across the parking lot from our hospital. He had told her that he knew she didn't have any money, so he couldn't fix her, but he could manage her pain. "We're going to treat the pain, not cure the problem," she remembered him saying. As long as this made it possible for her to work, that seemed reasonable. He said, "Normally, I'd do an MRI, but that's unaffordable," and so he wrote her a prescription instead:

300 mg Norco
5 mg Vicodin
1 mg Zofran

Three times a day for four years.

The language of pain is not unlike the language of addiction, muddied and hard to understand. It is all metaphor and subtext: pain comes in slices; addiction comes in tabs or (later) films, or is snorted or melted or injected. There is plenty of poetry in a spoon, its white heat. But that was another story.

✧ ✧ ✧

Let me tell you a different story. The woman came in on a Sunday. She had missed a step at church and was in terrible pain. She had a cane with four feet on it, pancake makeup, a dye job, a name like Carolyn, and a son, a man in his thirties whose role seemed to indicate—at least in part—that he had stayed behind to care for her.

The ER divided into two areas, loops cast wide around the nursing station, and was all about sight lines. A kind of oval, with a section for the fast-track techs, a section for nursing staff, and then small desks with dividers for the physicians to write up notes on their patients, *dispositions*, they called them.

We put Carolyn in room 17, on the fast-track side of the ER, because we weren't sure what else to do with her. All the trauma beds were taken, and she didn't lose consciousness during the fall. This part is important, because it means she would not get an EKG, or a CT scan, that perhaps we would X-ray her foot or back to rule out broken bones, perhaps wrap the affected area, and send her home.

"Divna, the physician assistant, will be with you in just a few minutes," I said.

✧ ✧ ✧

In our ER, we had lots of patients with lots of problems: the familiar gasping cough of chronic obstructive pulmonary disease, type 1 diabetics woozy from hypoglycemia, patients with neurological issues, Parkinson's or Lewy body dementia, people with psychiatric comorbidities to go along with their physical illness, but more often than not, our patients had everything, maybe half a dozen diseases or syndromes, reams of pages of workup, surgical notes, and carefully labeled I/Os (inputs and outputs) completed by nursing assistants from prior hospitalizations, old charts dating back decades, provided they were not new to our hospital system, which many of them were. In the latter case, we'd request old charts from other hospitals in an attempt to try to get to the bottom, the origin story, but this took time that we mostly did not have. Myla or Kathleen spent time tracking these sorts of things down, or else we would ask someone from admitting to help, or someone from records, anything that would help us better understand how and why we had gotten here, in this ER, today. We had old people and we had sick people, and most were both. Not everyone who was sick was old, but many of them were, and had been sick for decades, their diseases picked off one at a time by a sea of specialists: the endocrinologist for diabetes, maybe an orthopod for arthritis or a tricky hip or knee. The sleep physician for their CPAP machine, the PM&R specialist (that's physical medicine and rehabilitation, its own specialty now), the internist who specialized in geriatric populations, the dermatologist and the ophthalmologist, maybe a cardiologist or two.

✧ ✧ ✧

Kathleen and I had similarities: We were both the oldest, wanted to be paramedics, had brothers four years our junior, had dropped out of college at some point along the way.

Kathleen was mostly Irish, like me. We ate lunch together, or dinner, or whatever meal seemed appropriate given the time of day when we were at work. At this point, I wasn't great at sleep, so in a way, variable shifts suited me fine. Our brothers were both musicians; my brother had attended a special school for musicians, though lately he seemed to be balanced on the precipice of living and drinking. She was sleeping with her boyfriend and also a married paramedic with four kids. I slept with nobody. I swore off everything. At twenty-two, it was part of my new ascetic routine. I had stopped sleeping, stopped picking up the phone when my parents called asking me to do their dishes, or for money, or if I could take my dad to lunch. I had recently broken up with two boyfriends, one of whom I'd later marry and the other not, and was living in an inexpensive walk-up studio apartment that, at $695 a month, was still more than I could afford. I said no to buying groceries; no to the woman who asked me if I'd pick up her mail when she was out of town. I fired Lori, whom I was seeing for therapy only, but first told her no, that I didn't want to undergo psychoanalysis so she would be able to get her clinical hours in and complete her training program. No to my brother's requests for money or booze. I couldn't drink; I was on lithium, but I was about ready to quit that, too.

Divna, the PA, was hardened by her work at Mt. Sinai. Compared to our little community hospital, where she normally worked was busy and full of category I trauma cases, car crashes, drug seekers, gunshot wounds, and the kinds of rare childhood diseases that seemed to necessitate emergency surgery. She was *so* not interested in the cases at our hospital. I knew this because she said so about eleven times a day.

"This is ridiculous," she said, as she picked up the phone to page our lone on-call surgery resident once again, since she didn't answer the first time.

I handed her the paperwork for room 17. "Fall down go boom," I said. We said this in the ER all the time. "No loss of consciousness. Only, she says everything hurts. And she has a history."

Divna looked up at me. "Oh no," she said.

"Oh yes," I said. In dozens of old charts, it said she was allergic to everything except the pain meds she was looking for, which in this case included Dilaudid, a powerful IV-delivered narcotic, originally developed for end-stage cancer patients. Patients who weren't expected to make it three months.

❖ ❖ ❖

Kathleen maybe had a drug problem. And by "maybe," I meant "probably," something she explained to me as I coughed and inhaled her secondhand smoke by the transformer box in the hospital parking lot. We stood there, out of sight of security, a force comprised of poorly aging angry white men who yelled at everyone for loitering or smoking on hospital grounds, listening to the *click* and *thunk* of a loose transformer kick. She said she got migraines and also injured her back and the problem was more complex than I could imagine. And that the migraines couldn't be fixed by most of the drugs people use to fix migraines, so it needed to be fixed by something stronger instead. I didn't know any sick people, not like this. My brother did drugs at school, mushrooms mostly, maybe a little robotripping on cough syrup, and drank now, but Kathleen was talking about the hard stuff, probably narcotics.

"You know," she said, and like all those times I pretended to smoke in my Catholic all-girls high school parking lot just to be cool, I went along with it.

"Yeah," I said.

But really Kathleen had a pain problem: she had back pain from the accident, originally, and also pelvic pain, ovarian cysts, endometriosis. I knew what this looked like, intimately: I had a tendency to vomit at least once a month because of hormones and pelvic pain and would later be diagnosed with endometriosis, too. I got migraines. I was told I should take Advil for my period, that cramps were normal, which felt to me like offering a Band-Aid to a man hemorrhaging, the bandage swept away on a river of hot red blood. Years later, surgery would be offered, administered, and fail to fix my problem. I didn't know what to do, but had never considered anything stronger than what I had been allotted.

In the ER, we asked patients to qualify their pain but were taught not to offer or prompt unless it was clear that they were not going to understand what they'd been asked. Then: "Stabbing? Dull? How would you describe it? Does the pain move anywhere?"

✧ ✧ ✧

According to her records, Carolyn in room 17 had been in for foot pain, leg pain, arm pain, shoulder pain, groin pain, hip pain, back pain, neck pain, head pain. She had a history of fibromyalgia, of arthritis, of osteoporosis, of degenerative joint disease. Back in the room, I found her dressed in a hospital gown; she knew she was off to radiology. "Can you rate your pain on a scale of zero to ten, zero being no pain, and ten being the worst imaginable?" I asked. I asked this question twenty or thirty or fifty times a day.

"Ten," she whispered, the only ten so far that day, including the guy who cut off his own finger with a ten-inch chef's knife. I wrote it down.

Outside, in the hallway, Divna and her attending, Mark, discussed Carolyn's treatment plan.

"Irradiate the shit out of her," Mark said. "Then when the X-rays come back negative, give her a shot of Dilaudid and send her home." Mark was knowledgeable, experienced. He knew how to treat *these people* and their very specific needs without giving them a prescription for anything. That was what they were after more than anything else: the hope that they could get something longer-term, anything for pain.

✧ ✧ ✧

The information we collected appeared in an improvised log-book form, a list of our frequent fliers combined with another list of the drugs they asked for, all alphabetized. Carolyn was not on this list, nor was Kathleen, but we were not great at keeping track of our patients in this way. There was another computer log, but sometimes the secretaries entered the information incorrectly or the patient gave a false name. The best we could go on was how we *felt* about things, which seemed a suspicious science. I am not the kind of person who locates scientific esti-mations by gut feel, though something about some of these patients was enough to write a note in their file.

✧ ✧ ✧

Kathleen's pain extended to visits at emergency departments all over the city. Sts. Mary and Elizabeth, Rush, Advocate Lutheran General, St. Francis, Elmhurst Hospital, where she knew the schedule for Dr. Feelgood—this was what the nurses called him, a liberal prescriber, a guy who would write you ten or twenty or thirty Percocet without blinking. She explained her strategy over falafel at our favorite Middle Eastern restaurant closest to the hospital. At Pita Inn, you could get falafel for a couple of bucks, and they're open pretty much always, which is why half the restaurant is in scrubs at any given time. Kathleen said she had migraines; that part was true.

"Yeah," I said.

"Sometimes I go when I don't have one, though."

She knew what to say, what to do. She was a medical assis-tant, so people took her more seriously, or maybe less, depend-ing on the hospital. It varied, she said. So she didn't hit any one hospital too frequently; she had a logbook of her very own.

✧ ✧ ✧

When Carolyn came back from X-ray, the results were in: there was nothing wrong with her. Nothing. Sure, she had osteoarthritis, degenerative joint disease, but nothing that might have had to do with the fall. Nothing that would give her what she came for. Divna brought her the news.

"You bitch!" Carolyn screamed.

Divna charted, *calls PA a bitch, 2140.*

Divna and I hid in the break room for a little while after Carolyn had been discharged. We could go home, it was ten p.m., but neither one of us trusted the idea that Carolyn wouldn't be waiting up in the parking lot. They hadn't left yet but were on their way; her son, ever helpful, probable virgin, late twenty-something, helped her to the door, pushing the faceplate on the wall with his huge, meaty palm. She'll sit on the bench outside so that way he could bring the car around in front of the ambulance bay, and then he'll open the front passenger door for her, and her cane, her only evidence of disability, will slide up next to her hip.

✧ ✧ ✧

The next shift, we got another one. A young man, midtwenties, threw his back out moving a friend's couch, he said. He was in pain, didn't know what to do. And I bought it—he seemed like he was in pain. He gripped the painful part of his body, as we are socialized to do. He seemed genuine, not smart enough to ask for the hard stuff. Probably we could let him go with muscle relaxants—Flexeril—if we wanted.

The shift after that, another one still: a woman in her thirties, with children, a husband who didn't realize what part of her pain was real and which part was imagined. Another fibromyalgia case.

So we ran a tox screen, which lit up her file like a Christmas tree. Bingo. She was on narcotics, enough to make her high before she even arrived through our door.

✧ ✧ ✧

Years from now, I will park outside a Target, southwest of the city, on a weekday morning. I've taken the day off from work, and Kathleen's called me out of nowhere, and we haven't seen each other for years, but we've kept in touch through the usual channels, mostly birthday wishes on Facebook, the occasional Happy New Year text. In the parking lot, flattened paper cups mat and form paste on the ground; it's been raining on and off for the past few days, and in the deeper puddles you can see gasoline films coating the surface of the asphalt. We're meeting inside, up an escalator above a parking structure filled with cars, and then there she is, I think. She's a little heavier than her most recent Facebook photos, dressed in a gray sweatshirt with the neck cut out and a sports bra and leggings, sneakers. Her stomach pulls at her sweatshirt. There are two kids now, but she doesn't have either of them with her. She needed to see me, we needed to talk, she said. I live near the hospital where we used to work and occasionally drive past it on my way to my new job. So I text *miss you*s, *hope you're doing well.* She's been living down south and has now moved back home with her husband and their kids to her mother-in-law's house ten minutes from this Target. We get coffee inside and grab a cart.

"I have to tell you something," she said. I looked closely at her; her pupils were pinpoints. "I started heroin." She's going to rehab down in Florida, someone found her a spot, and she's leaving tomorrow, so we were going to spend our shopping excursion looking at bathing suits and sunscreen and pretending that everything is fine. Afterward, we hug, she said she'd write me, and I told her I'd write her. It'll be good, she said. Good to get clean.

✧ ✧ ✧

Kathleen pulled a quarter out of her pocketbook and deposited it into a slot to free one of the shopping carts. It was a Thursday, months later, after rehab and what followed. We had agreed to meet at an ALDI in her new neighborhood, close to the house her husband rented and moved their family into while she was in rehab. On top of his regular job in wholesale auto parts, he spent most weekends at Soldier Field, selling beer to football fans and concertgoers. They were about $15,000 in credit card debt, Kathleen had explained to me, and the number never seemed to get any smaller. She'd relapsed again, too.

Between the cost of housing, and food, they barely had enough left over to cover the monthly minimum. And since Kathleen couldn't work at a hospital or in health care anymore, she struggled to find something to do that worked around carefully timed doses of methadone, recovery meetings, and weekly outpatient therapy. She pulled out her keys to replace her pocketbook into her purse. Her Narcotics Anonymous chip dangled from her key chain. Ninety days sober. She'd agreed to meet me at this ALDI because she needed to go grocery shopping, and since it was attached to a mall, we could wander around and maybe get coffee afterward.

She wore her same sweatshirt with the neck cut out, sports bra, and patterned stretch pants. I pretended to be interested in salted almonds while she leaned against the cart and caught me up on what was going on in her life lately. I watched as a woman with a cart full of produce watched us, glaring at Kathleen at the casual mention of methadone. We were always having conversations like this in public places, it seemed. She'd tell

me about her latest relapse while shouting over the dressing
room divider at Target, or explain that her friends wanted her
to go out and do drugs with them. This kind of public display of
self didn't bother her. She couldn't afford to care about these
sorts of things, she once told me, but that wasn't quite it either.
It reminded me of a woman I knew, a former professor's daughter, who had a significant developmental disability that was hard
to catch at first glance. The daughter could be the secretary at
your dentist's office or in line behind you at the grocery store
and you wouldn't notice her disability. So she wore sports jer-
seys and sweatbands as a way to signal to outsiders to treat her
differently. Communicating information about Kathleen's drug
addiction in public spaces telegraphed a similar kind of meaning. This was it, she was telling anyone who would listen. This
was why she looked and dressed in this way, how come her hair
was unwashed and the way her sweatshirt pulled at the bulge of
her stomach that flopped over the waist of her stretch pants.
How she composed herself in public. Why she was buying groceries in the middle of the day and having difficulty figuring out
whether or not they could afford milk that week.

"I'll just throw it in here"—she motioned to the cart—"and
will take if out if we go over," she said.

A friend of hers had overdosed, she explained. He was dead
and it sucked and she hated him for it and she missed him.
Everyone figures out how to keep using and how to make the
best friends in rehab, she said, though she had gotten to know
him mostly through her dealer, who wasn't speaking to her
right now on account of the fact that she was on methadone.
Before methadone, she sold her Suboxone prescription to buy
drugs. Suboxone was good like that. Methadone, less so. And,
she wanted to remind me and the rest of aisle 4 who was listening, that she has always snorted heroin, never used needles, so

at least she didn't have to worry about locating and participating in a clean needle exchange.

At the register, both the SunnyD and the milk made the cut. She pushed the cart through the checkout line, and we bagged the groceries at the counter afterward, still talking. She had gotten a job at a salon part-time. Front desk, she said. You know. She answered the phones and swept hair and greeted clients as they walked in, for $10 an hour. She only had to go in a couple of days a week, and since she had befriended one of the stylists, her hair—cut and color—was cheap, almost free.

Out in the mall, we walked from one end to the other and back again. I kept trying to think of something to make our time last longer, though both of us had run out of things to say. We passed Rainbow and DOTS and Gloria Jean's Coffees; there was no Starbucks.

"Remember all those patients who were our frequent fliers?" I asked suddenly. I was grasping at something, anything to get her to talk to me more.

I didn't know why I needed this, except that it seemed like the more I spoke with old friends I had met when I was younger and less put together, the further away they seemed to appear. Like a perspective drawing, a shadowbox, an apple in front of the man with the bowler hat. The closer I came, the less things made sense. Here she was, heaving groceries into her family's car, deciding if ALDI-branded milk—fresh, not powdered—was an unknowable luxury at $3.99. Trying to make sense of where she was and how far she'd come. How Tom needed to make more money and how he had threatened to leave her and take their children, a boy (two) and a girl (six, almost seven). There simply wasn't any space for where she needed to be. How sorry she was that any of this—and when she says *this*, I'm not sure if she means the drugs or her family, but then of course she means both—ever happened; if the accident had never happened, if she had seen another doctor, one who found a way to give her the MRI necessary to see the problem and the surgery required to fix it—maybe she would have been a totally different person, living a totally different life. I want to believe this. I do.

Failures in Communication

The wife is crying again. She can't stop, won't stop, and she's no amateur about it either: the sobs come in huge gasps in a way that makes it seem as though they're stacking on top of one another. If she doesn't take a real breath soon, I worry she'll pass out, though admittedly this is the place for it.

We're in her husband's room, a two-person space that holds just him right now. Every day, the group of us come in to talk to her, to round on her husband. Three medical students, whose names and faces appear to rotate almost weekly (though they generally spend at least three or four weeks on this floor), two or sometimes three interns, one senior resident, one attending, the nursing case manager, Mary, and me. I'm a bioethics student assigned to shadow their floor, an ICU step-down unit in Pittsburgh, where I am, for twenty hours a week, following the group from patient to patient, listening to rounds. I'm a graduate student in the writing department, too, but I'm not here in this capacity. I'm supposed to be a totally quiet, impartial observer, nearly invisible, which is fine, so I stand in the back and don't talk much. This particular senior resident has taken to introducing all of us, something I haven't seen much so far. But the woman, the wife, is sobbing in a way that is making all of us uncomfortable. We're not used to emotion here, not in that sense. Something is clinical, off, seems to create pathology. She is blond and matronly in a schoolteacher kind of way, a contrast to her husband, who is all angles, thin in the elbows and knees.

The room faces west, has two beds, side by side, one shared bath, and two curtains in between. The husband is sitting partially upright in bed, reclining at an angle that seems like it must be awkward or uncomfortable, but when a med student asks if she can adjust it, he waves her off. "It's fine, it's fine," he says. Though it is almost certainly not.

The wife's crying seems to reverberate through the small space, amplifying the sound. It's my first day with this particular patient, this team. I've spent the better part of the month shadowing at an ICU in another hospital, where patients have complex medical issues that seem unlikely to be resolved, so the ethical issues are mostly worked out in headspace: Do we do this treatment, or that? Who is the decision maker? the doctors ask. Has she been informed about the procedure? (Or more likely, has the family?) The nurses move with precision, act mostly independently with minimal support from physicians. There, the patients are mostly asleep, sedated, or unresponsive, and so the machines that power them seem more human than the humans themselves. In ICU step-down, here, patients are responsive, awake, alert, not generally hooked to a ventilator, but nevertheless very sick. This is the hardest part for patients and families to understand: that their loved one may still die, even though he seems fine, able to communicate, awake, alert, like here, like today. It is well understood that ICU nurses talk to attending physicians, physical therapists, occupational therapists, other nurses, respiratory therapists, residents, interns. Patients are not on this list. In this unit, though, nurses don't seem to be able to stop talking to patients, even if they want to: most everyone is lonely.

The patient in bed 1, by the window, is immunocompromised. The patient has undergone chemotherapy for his cancer and is currently in remission, but his immune system is weak and he may still die from a secondary infection. He was transferred from the hospital in Morgantown. This happens a lot: transfers

from Morgantown or other hospitals in West Virginia. There
are more resources here in Pittsburgh, more options. There
are sixty-three hospitals in the entire state of West Virginia, and
only one Level I trauma center: West Virginia University Hospitals. The *s* appended to the name means only that there are
several buildings, not necessarily separate, independent facilities. Level I means that the hospital has resources, trappings to
cover the worst types of emergencies: round-the-clock access to
a CT scanner or MRI machine, round-the-clock lab results, and
at the very least, helicopter service to receive urgent patients
from other facilities. On a countrywide map of trauma centers,
holes in the map appear where no trauma center exists. In the
western half of the United States, patches of purple are missing
from the map, but there are fewer people living there. Most
states on the eastern seaboard are colored in solid, but there is
a huge gray gap over places like Pocahontas County and else-
where in West Virginia. When I worked at a Level II trauma center near Chicago and took classes to become an EMT, I didn't
know that Level IV trauma centers existed. Even Level III, to
me, seems below the resources necessary to save a life, especially
if no other hospitals are nearby to take the transfer in complicated cases like these.

Most of the hospitals in West Virginia do not have expensive
equipment or machinery; few of them even seem to get a Level
IV designation. Pocahontas Memorial Hospital, for example,
is the only hospital in Pocahontas County, West Virginia, and
has just 25 beds compared with University of Pittsburgh Medical Center's 4,733; it carries no trauma designation at all. So
patients like this one come for additional treatment, resources,
from small hospitals and from larger ones. Though the hospital
in Morgantown is Level I, more research is done at UPMC, so
the doctors here can send samples of his illness to the lab to

get it cultured, to see which drugs might respond best to the disease.

They've cultured this man's cells twice so far, once at his previous hospital and once here. The team is still waiting for the results from UPMC's lab, so they're using the previous hospital's results to treat the fungus growing inside him. He is in his late fifties or early sixties, and has an appearance that has begun to seem a little peculiar. While his wife snuffles softly in the background, the medical student presents his case, explains that the reason for his admission is that he has been receiving treatment for his cancer, but that he now has a secondary infection, a fungus in his nose that has grown behind the orbit of his right eye. Nobody is sure what it is that's growing inside him, or what it might do if it gets worse, so he has neutropenic precautions for his room. We are supposed to wear masks when in the room with him. Any little thing can set it off, a microbe, some pollen. As a rule, patients with absolute granulocyte counts under 1,500 milliliters should have neutropenic precautions in place, which means masks but not gowns, no fresh fruit or flowers in the room. Unlike other types of precautions, we are trying to avoid getting *him* sick instead of him getting us or other patients sick. This is why he's alone for the moment, the other side of the curtain left unoccupied.

"So there has been some protrusion," the med student says. And there has: the patient's right eye bulges, pushed just beyond its socket's limits, in a way that makes him almost a gargoyle. I am told we are wired for facial symmetry, as humans, and so this kind of disruption feels abrupt, startling. Developmental biologists have suggested that facially symmetrical people have superior genetics, and staring at this man's face is a kind of hiccup in an otherwise aseptic, starched environment. He can't close his eyelid completely over the bulging eye, so he turns away from the light at the window to sleep at night.

When I learned to be an EMT, in class, we'd role-play how to talk to patients, but it was never about the patients themselves, only their illness. Our relationship with the patient only lasted as long as was needed, to get the information out of them before we got to the hospital. Necessary information went into the chart. Everything else that didn't relate to the diagnosis—what the patient thought, perhaps, or what his nephew liked to say—didn't merit discussion. In emergency situations, it was not uncommon to cover the patient's face with a mask within seconds of meeting, especially if the ambulance had been called for something like respiratory distress.

There are three bags of IV antifungal and antibiotic medications hanging at his bedside. He is wearing his own pajamas. Something I learn quickly: patients who wear their own pajamas are in some way surrendering to the long stretch of the hospital stay before them and the acres behind. He knows what it's like to be here, knows what kind of experiences may be expected, what kinds of questions we will likely ask. When I worked in an emergency department, patients told us it was like Vegas: there are no doors or windows, nobody knows what day it is, and we're always open. Hospital time is like this, different from regular time.

There is variability in the nursing staff, too. The day-shift nurses are different from the second shifters, who are in turn different from the night staff. I used to work second or third shift in my past life, never first, so this group of nurses is different from the kind I know best. They are prickly, protective of their patients, and irritated by the docs' presence. The nurse assigned to the patient today is B, twenties, thin, brunette, with a ponytail. She does not want to listen to the staff present on the patient. She does not have this kind of time. A nurse's responsibilities extend far beyond having to listen to doctors relay information to one another that the nurse already knows and will both have to read the chart later and chart on the fact that the chart was read. You can tell B is good at her job, that she works hard to show that her patients are her top priority, in spite of the problems that the med students and residents bring to disrupt her pattern of care. But the man in his pajamas is what is cementing us in this time, this space. He is the only one really here.

This patient—we'll call him R—is stationed at the end of the hall, last door on the right, far away from the room where the docs do their charting, phone calls, and order medications. Inside their windowless Red Team room, the delegate of docs hopes for *results*, a way to make sense of what is happening on the other side of the door, in the hallways, in their patients' rooms. They order tests, pre-round on patients by discussing the cases in the privacy of the room before venturing out onto the floor, and have a way of considering the care and treatment of their patients inside the room that makes most things feel uncertain. It is not that they do not know. Some things they do know. But much of it is murky.

Our senior resident is male, with a Midwestern accent, and friendly in a powerfully effervescent way. He has a smile that seems as though he is about ready to tell you good news all the time, even when he is struggling to explain something to a patient or the patient's family. He has instituted a new policy whereby the med students and interns here are expected to come up with a new fact about the patient every day and use that information as part of how they introduce him or her. When the med students and residents fail to do this, they are playfully chided for their failure, generally in front of the patient, some of whom helpfully opt to supply their own fact for the physician's benefit. When an intern goes missing, someone inevitably jokes that he or she quit, and the team laughs. For the most part, we laugh a lot, even when someone is dying in the room adjacent to our jokes. Levity keeps us moving, edging off despair at the likelihood that even if most of these patients get better and go home, someone else will arrive to take their place. It's no surprise that burnout is one of the most common and debilitating issues for physicians, or that so many I know have elaborate hobbies, ways to keep the immediacy of their patients' mortality at bay.

Two of the interns are counting down the hours until they are no longer interns. I know this because I overhear them discussing their soon-to-be new lives as full-fledged residents, where their rotations will take them. This floor, despite being designed for a crew of internal medicine physicians, is known for challenging patients, challenging problems. Everybody has three or five or eight or ten serious problems; the medical issues are complex and for the most part interesting, and sometimes everyone wants to crowd into a room just so they can get a glimpse of the patient's story or wound. "This is a teaching hospital," someone will inevitably announce, generally when trying to get a patient's permission to let students or interns listen to their unusual heart rhythm or an opportunity to look closely at an obscure neurological finding. The patient at the end of the hall, R, is interesting because he offers one of those obscure findings.

Medicine is full of slogans. A common phrase in medical practice is "when you hear hoofbeats, think horses"; the most obvious explanation is the likeliest. But patients like R are all zebra or unicorn, mythical beasts of disease with no known explanation, cause, or cure. The intern assigned to R is completing a preliminary year in internal medicine before she'll move on to her chosen specialty, which in her case is neurology, so she and the medical student assigned to her spend a lot of time with a flashlight in R's eyes, hoping that the way his eyes move was neither fluke nor sleight of hand but neurologic pathology, findings that can be charted.

The team is responsible for up to fifteen patients, but during this week they hover around a census of just eight. Most of their patients need their own rooms because of isolation precautions, and as many as a third or more aren't rounded on personally due to an inability for the patient to respond, or else have additional circumstances that make rounding on them difficult or undesirable, so the cases are discussed in the hall. Notably, patients with psych/med comorbidities tend to be rounded on in the hall rather than in front of the patients. Unlike the University of Iowa hospital where I used to work, there is no med/psych ward here, and it turns out that nobody at UPMC seems to have access to patient files at Western Psychiatric Institute and Clinic (WPIC), making care for those patients even more complex than one might initially imagine. Furthermore, I keep hearing that the interns and med students are "uncomfortable" with psych meds, so medicines tend to get discontinued or started without much fanfare.

This first week, I keep getting introduced as a philosophy student, which is wrong. I clarify the introduction: I'm here in a clinical bioethics capacity, here to just shadow and watch medical decision-making, but it's several days in before the resident seems to change what is said. Sometimes I am not introduced but am merely one of the students, which may imply medical students, although I'm the only one not in a short coat, so some of the patients seem to eye me suspiciously (or maybe that's just me).

Speaking with the interns and medical residents before and

after rounds, I find out one is terrified of drawing blood but wants more practice, and I consider offering my arm as practice because I have good veins, am an easy draw. I have trained a bunch of techs to draw blood using my arm, but I think it's probably not quite right here, so I smile and nod instead.

✧ ✧ ✧

Two doors down from R, the patient is dwarfed by her bed. She is a Somali refugee and was admitted because her gallbladder needed to be removed, an emergency cholecystectomy. According to the intern, she doesn't speak English, only Kizigua (or Chizigua), a language that nobody on the language line can speak. The husband speaks Swahili and Kizigua, so the senior resident dials the language line and speaks English to the translator, who speaks Swahili to the patient's husband, who speaks Kizigua to the patient. Just a few questions take almost half an hour. The connection to the Swahili translator isn't great, so the patient's husband keeps asking the translator to repeat what he is saying.

"Can you ask her how she's feeling?" he asks. Then a pause, then the translation into Swahili, then the translation into Kizigua. Her eyes are wide, unblinking. Is she in pain?

Where I used to work, we never used the language line. Probably not ethical to use the care provider as the translator, or the family member, as in the case of the patient who only speaks Kizigua, but what choices exist in situations like these? Translating English seems difficult enough.

✧ ✧ ✧

The fungus inside R's sinuses is *invasive*, which means it's attacking the blood vessels, mucosa, even bone. The condition is called acute fulminant invasive fungal sinusitis, meaning it started out of seemingly nowhere, just a growth inside this man's nasal cavity.

Left unchecked because of his immunocompromised status, the fungus has spread rapidly. This is the worst kind of fungal sinusitis; it is aggressive, appears from nowhere, and has an appetite for orbits of eyes, blood vessels, and brain parenchyma—that is, neurons and glial cells, the functional parts of the brain. So far he seems more or less neurologically intact, though the scans and numbers seem to indicate everything is growing at an exponential rate. The team calls consults, but nobody seems to know whether or not R will survive: over 50 percent of these types of patients do not.

Outside his room, in the low roar of the hallway, the team is trying to figure out whether or not to present his case in front of him today. "Remember to talk about what has *changed* for now," the senior resident says. When presenting a case, it's easy to get bogged down in minutiae, to recite a lengthy string of numbers that tells the team about the patient's case but doesn't really inform or change what the patient or the family know. They cling to minute, insignificant changes that are not statistically significant, tiny dips or peaks in the numbers recited by some medical student. The pre-rounding takes place in the team room at the other end of the hallway prior to the start of actual rounds, where the med student or intern can practice what he or she will say in front of the patient so as to not startle anyone unnecessarily. Since some of these patients are among the sickest in this section of the hospital (yet they're still conscious), everything that needs to be explained about their case is in the delivery: nuance, tone, meter, facial expression. Today, R's results have come back, and the fungus that has been identified is different from the one they found at the previous hospital. This means that he'll get more antifungals, more antibiotics. It's possible that two different fungi are growing in this man's nasal cavity. That's the assumption going into the meeting this morning. It makes treatment more complex, the outlook a little less bright. The lab and the clinical mycologist and pharmacist have made some suggestions, and it is up to the internal medicine team to implement them. Starting R on these new drugs may have lasting effects, though all of them are more mild than just dying from this invasive fungus.

When the intern explains all of this to R and his wife, they nod. "Okay," R says. "Whatever you think is best." This is the best and also the worst response; there's no real way to ascertain whether or not he is satisfied with the explanation and the plan of treatment or if he has simply given up.

❖ ❖ ❖

Our team starts to switch the following day. The teams here are set up in a way that makes it so there is always overlap between the various groups: nobody is ever entirely new. There are pluses and minuses to this system. It's good because it means that patients with complex cases requiring many days of hospitalization get a variety of opinions: the treatment plan from one physician may be different from someone else's. The problems come in continuity of care, in making sure no mistakes are made when the patients are switched from one team to another. To avoid having an entirely new team every time a new rotation begins, there is a delay: the senior resident switches a week before the rest of the team does, thereby giving the rest of the group time to relay important information about the patient to the new senior resident before they too switch to another floor. So one day there is someone else leading our group on rounds.

Our new senior resident, M, has long curly hair and a penchant for cute shoes, mostly flats, which seems sensible, a fact that is reflected in the way she practices medicine. She smiles a lot, wears dresses, and has both an easygoing way of chatting up her patients and a tendency to forget her stethoscope in the team room or hanging from a patient's IV pole. When it comes to the patient's privacy, she is protective: those who become overly agitated or confused by a huge team are offered smaller groups of people, more familiar faces, fewer changes. This is both a boon and a possible annoyance: the patients don't have to see as many practitioners, but the team doesn't get to see as many cases either. Some patients get rounded on in the hall or are only seen by the attending or the senior resident and the med student or intern assigned to the case.

Having a new team feels weird. Everyone does things differently. The acting intern seems anxious, and even tells me as much. She has been away from patient care for two years, having completed an MS in clinical research in the meantime. The evidence of this fact is all there: she is awkward around patients, struggles with a flimsy gown when abiding by contact precautions, doesn't ask for permission when listening to patients' hearts or carotid arteries, shows palpable anxiety in reading a completely normal EKG to the resident. She lurches for patients, grabbing at them. She's child-size, and nothing is made for her shape; even the small gloves are too big for her hands. She's messing up things that I don't even think to do incorrectly, and I'm not sure why. Everything seems slightly turned. The other med student seems a strange mix of sweaty and cavalier. Our third is missing, still out.

Our new resident doesn't introduce anyone, a departure from the last resident's behavior. It feels wrong somehow, but maybe it's just me thinking that the patients are looking at me sans coat, wondering why I'm there.

❖ ❖ ❖

Two interns, one resident, three medical students, and an attending, female, who appears for one of the days this week. Much
of the banter in the early part of the week consists of discussion about whether and when the attending will appear. Finally,
when she does appear, everyone is on their best behavior. The
med students crowd her, ask lots of questions. She is a celebrity,
someone to be feared. According to the Pitt med school website, she directs the standardized patient program, and I want to
ask her about it, but since we're being timed by someone from
Quality Improvement to see how long it takes us to do rounds
and which parties need to be involved, I shut up and stand in
the back; there will be time to ask later.

This way of doing things, in which room to room is timed
(not surprisingly) isn't popular with anyone, except maybe some
of the nurses and of course the administration. The nursing staff
is annoyed with the fact that they have to round on patients and
listen to the "teaching moments" that the residents and attendings offer to the med students and interns. In the team room,
M, our resident, tries to justify the change to the new rounding
system to her team. "The more time we spend in here, the less
time we spend at bedside."

It seems like a strange statement to make, but I kind of
understand its implication. They want the team to spend less
time discussing cases in the hall, use patient-friendly language
when talking to patients at bedside, and be less wasteful of
the nurses' time. They're supposed to spend ten minutes per
patient, which seems alarming. The woman who is following
us and taking notes keeps looking at her phone, her portable
stopwatch. Everyone wants to present in the hall.

"I don't feel comfortable presenting at bedside," one of the
med students explains, but it's because she has to learn two

languages, one for the patients and one for medicine. She's almost mastered the medical language; learning the one for patients in front of the patients is almost too much. In the case of patient-friendly language, there is some attention paid to managing anxiety—of the patients or the family members. In one case, a woman with rheumatoid arthritis (RA) who has been in and out of the hospital quite a bit, the husband is hypervigilant. The doctors appear to be omitting certain language they use with other patients. The patient herself is fine with various changes to her regimen, but when the husband is there—and he is always there—they don't say everything. He assumes the worst. So the information sometimes is incomplete, or they wait to tell the husband until they are sure they are going to do this procedure or that. I assume that in some—perhaps many—ways this must affect patient care. Is making them the last to know helping or hurting them? Where is the line? I think of the study that said recently that interns only spend 13 percent (or less) of their time with patients and 40 (or maybe 60) percent of the time sitting in front of a computer. Yes, they have to enter the orders, write the notes—but is anyone actually bothering to explain the ramifications of a certain treatment to a patient?

✧ ✧ ✧

Back in R's room, down the hall, last door on the right, a roommate has joined him. R's still on neutropenic precautions for now, but so is his roommate. Usually neutropenic precautions are reserved for one patient per room, but the team has decided that he's not likely to infect himself any more than he already has, so he's gotten a roommate, a guy who mows lawns for a country club outside Pittsburgh. When we enter the room, he makes eye contact.

"Why, hello, all!" he says. Clearly nobody has told him this is a hospital.

"Good morning, Mr. P—we'll be with you in just a minute; we need to talk to your neighbor first," the senior resident explains.

"Oh, okay!" he says. He is possibly the happiest guy I've ever seen in a hospital gown. His eyes sparkle; one of his front teeth is missing. The senior resident makes eye contact with one of the interns, raises an eyebrow, then smiles. His chart says he has a mild intellectual disability. All of his fingers have been surgically reattached following an incident with his ride-on lawnmower.

On the other side of the curtain, our patient's family is decidedly less cheery. The wife looks at me, looks at the team, as if she doesn't recognize any of us, even though we've been coming into her husband's room every day for weeks. She purses her lips. Hoping for news.

"So," the senior resident says.

"*So?*" she snaps.

"We have some new results from the tests we've completed on your husband," the intern says. She has rehearsed, precisely, this language, this turn of phrase, in the Red Team room just a few minutes before. She had a discussion with the senior resident, how to phrase things in such a way that nobody will panic, but so that everything is truthful, precise. She tells them that there is another fungus that is apparently growing much faster than before, that the scans suggest that it may require *surgical management* or that he could potentially lose his eye. When the intern is done, she waits for the patient or his family to say something.

The room is quiet. There are no beeping machines, even;

he was removed from telemetry days ago and the only evidence of his hospital stay is marked in the IV pole parked next to his bed and the clear plastic port inserted into the back of his hand, a thin, ragged slice of clear tape holding everything down. R's neighbor on the other side of the curtain is quiet, too. R examines the tape on the back of his hand, smooths it down with his free hand, aligns the hairs on the back of his forearm so they all go the same direction.

"Do you have any questions?" the resident wants to know.

"No," he says. "Not now."

❖ ❖ ❖

The woman in bed 2, two rooms down from R, is dying. She is eighty-seven years old and has congestive heart failure. She has been dying for weeks, months, maybe years now, but nobody has told her. She knows everything is smeared with an excruciating slowing, that it's harder to catch her breath. She was recently started on oxycodone for pain, but it's also a medication that puts a damper on her breathing. There is a wedding in October she hopes to attend, but it does not seem likely she will make it that far. The family has not been in to see her much. The medical staff keep trying to wean her off the oxygen, but she needs more and more; she is switched from a nasal cannula to a face mask and back again, and then back again. The nurses say she is really nice, *just the sweetest lady*, I hear the case manager explain to hospice over the phone.

Perhaps because she is *so sweet*, nobody has really explicitly discussed that she is dying. This is one of those strange conundrums. If you are too sweet or a pain in the ass, nobody is going to tell you the truth. And even if you are none of these things, but just a regularly compliant patient, it's also possible that they will forget to tell you that you are dying.

This may be something of an exaggeration. I think on some level, she must be aware. And there was a family meeting a few days ago, one I did not attend, though the summary was something like "Let's make her comfortable," per the resident who did. I want to attend a family meeting but feel awkward asking. It seems not my place, and with some meetings there are so few people in attendance, I wouldn't want to be mistaken for an actual bioethicist.

The patient jokes a lot with hospital staff. The nurses say she reminds them of Betty White. Which part, I wonder, as she even kind of resembles the woman, if in a slightly larger form.

✧ ✧ ✧

The med students don't appear every day; sometimes they go to grand rounds or have research-related meetings or daylong seminars that involve the cases they're seeing in the hospital. I am fascinated by them: their movements, their strange behaviors, the totally inappropriate things they say to patients and their families, the urgency in which the residents or interns rush to correct them. Right now there are three of them: two men and one woman, the woman the acting intern, or AI, some special distinction for an almost-fourth-year med student who is considering the specialty. One of the two guys keeps trying to get me to apply to medical school. It's distracting when I'm trying to observe, and I'm not sure of the reason. I don't think he's trying to flirt with me. I guess I am applying, significantly later than the typical applicant, if I can score well enough on the MCAT, though the whole thing still seems kind of absurd. I think at least two of the med students I'm following each have at least one physician parent. I can probably count on one hand the number of times I saw a doctor as a kid. My birth was overseen by a midwife, albeit in a hospital; my mom walked there, had me, and then walked home.

When I got my first hospital job, the nurse practitioner in employee health drew half a dozen vials because I couldn't answer any of the questions on the form I'd been given: hep B? TDAP? MMR? Flu? Blood type? I thought I got the MMR vaccine for school and I had chicken pox as a kid, but wasn't sure about the rest. When the titers came back, she called me down to her basement office, frowned, then inoculated me for everything. Medicine, even the idea of it, the thing, seems far away. When I call my dad and ask him for the amount of his social security income so I can put it on the form (how quaint that they ask for parental data when you register for the MCAT), he doesn't understand. Why are they asking for this information? he wants to know. I'm too naive to realize that you can study for it in advance, can't afford the study books in any case, so I take it cold, and do about as well as one might expect, which is poorly. Then I listen to the med students talk among themselves during rounds, and it feels like a race I've already lost, the chip still laced to my foot. These people have been doctors forever, since before any of us were born. They have been programmed to be doctors: the way they talk about patients—instead of *to* patients, like nurses do—has been inside them for years. I want to be a doctor, but I can't be a doctor. I am a tech, an EMT, maybe a nurse if I can take some prerequisites and get into the program at the community college, though these programs have gotten more and more competitive as time has gone on. This is all clear, somehow.

✧ ✧ ✧

The team seems more at ease this week, more jokey, though they vacillate between the overly formal and the overly informal. There is some hostility on the day-nurse front. B, whom we've

met before, hates the acting intern specifically and medical students in general, but the acting intern is oblivious, so it seems
the hatred is wasted on her. B is fiercely loyal to her patients,
and is trying her best to keep the med students from killing
anybody, but due to her perceived position, the med students
ignore her or treat her as if she is not as knowledgeable, even
though she is the one taking care of "their" patients. One morning, one of the nurses starts presenting the case, then apologizes
and stops, because this is *something that doctors do*. The resident
smiles, laughs, urges her on, and she continues. In the ICU, at
the other hospital, nurses routinely present on the patient; they
probably know more about his or her care than the intern does,
anyway.

But the roles are highly specific here in ICU step-down;
any deviation is seen as a kind of treason. One nursing "slipup"
can be okayed somehow, though it has to be "okayed" by the
one with the highest authority in the room. The med students
on ICU step-down don't know anything, so how are they going
to learn to behave appropriately with nursing staff? The acting intern dismisses them without realizing; the nurses corner
me to tell me they "hate—absolutely hate—medical students.
They're useless!" I try to smile and shrug and look apologetic
without saying anything, but they know I used to work as a
tech in a teaching hospital and I understand exactly what they
mean. I even sat for the entry exam for nursing school some
years back at the community college near my house, and I think
about trying for it again. It makes me wonder how these spats
affect patient care, or if any of the nurses would go far enough
to purposely undermine a medical decision, or just undermine,
even, the med student's suggestions. I'm guessing the latter is
done more frequently than not, for the patients' sakes. The
ethical implications of the relationship between med students

and nurses seem potentially problematic at best; at worst, we are harming patients, one medical student at a time.

✧ ✧ ✧

Four doors down from R, a patient has been classified as a "wander risk," so they've taped a photo of the patient to his door with his name and room number. Maybe a violation of patient privacy, but they're also trying to keep him on the floor, so it's a careful balance. When he complains about the sign, they take it down. He is lucid enough to care about such things. The patient is in his seventies and presents with a GI bleed. Everyone has a different opinion about the patient. Although he's strong enough to not be hospitalized on this floor, nobody seems to know what to do with him. Occupational Therapy has come in to do a KELS evaluation on him, an assessment to see if he's able to perform basic living skills, and the medical student assigned to the case has asked him a lot of questions, as has the resident. According to the med student, he just wants to go home, though he might not be entirely lucid. Psych wants to have him sent to a nursing home. They don't think he can consent to treatment, to anything, citing his "lacking capacity."

He is sleepy when we walk in, but it might be the Seroquel talking. The resident wants to ask him some questions. "Mr.——, would you come back to the hospital if you started bleeding again?"

"No."

"What would you do if your apartment caught on fire?"

He looks at her, then at the rest of us, incredulous. "I'd get out and call 911!"

In the hall, we stand in a circle. "Look," the acting intern says. "I don't think it's a question of him *lacking capacity*. I think he just wants to go home."

Our case manager, Mary, nods. "Sometimes patients just want to go home, even if it means they'll die at home alone. Does he have family?"

"Nobody who can take him. One sister had a stroke, another got a kidney recently. None of these people are interested in having him live with them. Visiting, yes. But no permanent solution." Everyone frowns, nods, makes noncommittal noises.

A week later, and he's still here, undergoing guardianship. The competency hearing is Monday. Is he getting the care he wants or needs? I can't say.

✧ ✧ ✧

The patient on the other side of R's curtain has changed again; he's now a sixty-four-year-old male with a history of hep C contracted through IV drug use, alcohol abuse, and cirrhosis. He won't make eye contact with any of the docs when they enter his room. He needs a liver transplant but is not eligible for one unless he stops drinking. This is an ethical problem, maybe, but also a practical one. The case manager on our team, Mary, worked in organ allocation for many years. She tells me privately, in the hall, that she is no longer an organ donor.

"They'll give you another one," Mary explains, if you burn through the first one. "I've seen them give organs to people who are going to fail." She is not against organ donation, but until the distribution is *more fair* (I don't stop to ask her what she means by this), she wants her family to decide for her. "Maybe they can meet them or something. See what kind of person is getting them," she says. In the meantime, she's removed "organ donor" from her driver's license.

I think about this for a while. There are various issues. The other candidate for a liver on our floor is a woman in her fifties who has supposedly stopped drinking but is probably addicted to narcotics, based on the information on her chart and the rate she burns through them. "I'm just here to get my belly tapped," she says to anyone who will listen; her belly has distended from the fluid—the official term is ascites—that has accumulated in between her organs from cirrhosis of the liver.

The male patient gets counseling, begrudgingly speaks with the nutritionist, his fluids are rebalanced, and he is released to the outside, promising he will quit drinking so he can be put on a transplant list.

Many of the patients who are really sick return to us, over and over again. We'll see him again, a few weeks later maybe, still drinking but cutting back, he promises. I see the same names repeating with each week that I'm here. Like a catch-and-release program, they return to us, again and again.

✧ ✧ ✧

On Monday, Labor Day, we're missing the medical students, so the team is smaller, and it's the outgoing residents' last day, so the mood seems marked by levity. "Oh, we're not going to make any changes to anyone's care plan *today*." Makes me wonder about continuity of care, about whether patients end up with more days inpatient during times when their physician is being switched out for someone else in teaching hospitals like this one.

We have new interns, two women, who start on Tuesday. The dynamic has shifted yet again on the floor, though I'm not exactly sure how. The senior resident makes some addenda, some corrections. Mostly it is in the form of making the new interns more personable, less automatic, robotic. The resident explains that they need to present in front of the patient and include him or her in their assessment, rather than pretending the patient isn't there, as is usually the case in situations like these. Oh, they say. Okay.

❖ ❖ ❖

Inside this room, the next one down from R, everyone wears gowns and gloves. I feel like we should probably be wearing masks, too, since the patient, a man whose age is hard to identify (though trached, he speaks and can cough up sputum as if he doesn't have a tracheostomy), has pneumonia, though I don't say anything.

The patient is flanked by all the contraptions of his medical life: ventilator, isolation stethoscope, nasogastric tube. He has had seven liters of fluid drained from his abdomen the day before. There is some talk in medicalese—the intern presents the case and then a statement is made by the resident—that this kind of complication is common in people in the *later ends of the disease.* This news stops the wife, who has been sitting there in gloves and a gown, her gloved hand pressed to her mouth. She is in her early or mid-sixties and is not entirely sure how to parse this information, it is clear. The expression on her face is mostly unreadable. It seems like the use of the word *end* is what is stopping her.

"How bad is his liver?"

"It's hard to quantify," the resident says. He is trying to say nothing.

She presses again for some kind of quantifiable response.

"I'm sorry, I don't really have a good answer," he says. "Some patients do live with this stage of liver disease for a long time; some are able to get transplants, but that's not an option, as you know, with your husband."

"Thank you," she says, though she is not really thanking anyone.

In the hall, the senior resident sighs a little. We're all stand-ing there, looking at him. He could reassure her, he tells us, but it seems maybe unethical.

What responsibility do physicians have to inform patients and family members of patients of their disease and where they are in the disease? How do you inform patients of their disease process? But the resident doesn't know what to say, and neither does anyone else.

One morning R seems to be better. Not substantively better, not "I can go home now" better, but better enough that the pro-trusion has stopped, that he is no longer having his face ripped in half by the fungi lurking beneath the bones of his face. In young people, the bones of the face have not ossified, are still malleable. This is generally accepted knowledge, but what the non-medical public does not know is that initial ossification still takes place up to age twenty-five, that bone tests can only be used to estimate one's age, but not overtly determine it, that everyone is aging at a different rate. I wonder what this means for our patient's bone age, if the fungus has disrupted the ossi-fication process—something that goes on constantly after age twenty-five, whereby the bones are rebuilt, cell by cell—in this part of his body, like tree rings.

But the news is good, the fungus has stopped eating every-thing in its path, and the resident suggests that if he can get it operated on, it may be possible to spare R's eye. The wife holds her breath a minute, then lets it out, a puff of air. She says noth-ing. The resident is careful with her speech; it *may be possible.* It *may be an option.*

His sight has been going in and out in his right eye for days now, probably from the advancing mass pressing on his optic nerve. This is part of what the almost-neurology-resident and the med student are looking for in shining a flashlight in his face every day: to see if this seemingly temporary damage is permanent. It may be, and it may not be. But the multitude of drugs dangling from his IV pole seem to be working, at least for now. He is on antifungals, antibiotics, a cocktail cooked specifically for him by the clinical pharmacy team, the clinical mycologist, the team of interns surrounding his bedside, some in short coats, indicating their student status, others in long ones. R's IV pump beeps: it's done; the bag needs to be switched again. The AI presses the CANCEL button frantically with her child-size hand, but it keeps going; the alarm has been set off. B, who is assigned to R as his nurse again today, reaches over, turns the pump off, and ejects the spent cartridge with one hand, then walks out into the hall to get a replacement from the dispensary refrigerator. Two more pin numbers and a fingerprint later, she has a new bag in her hand, coded with R's name: last name, first; patient ID number, room number, bed number. She snaps it in, checks the line for kinks, and all of us are suddenly quiet, listening as the pump begins to whir and click.

The Line
for
Cookies
Starts Here

"You ready?" my new boss asked. On the way down to the conference, I'd found out a little more about Christine: she had three kids, was from the southwest side of the city—tiny identical brick bungalows from the fifties, a split-level or two, home to firefighters, police officers, teachers, people who owned their own businesses. She had a bunch of siblings who all still lived nearby. She had a PhD in microbiology; her husband was also a scientist. They lived on the North Shore now, in a house that they had bought a few years ago, though she was already eyeing moving farther north, into a more exclusive neighborhood where her running club met and ran. Her car felt like the sort of kid-infused disaster of modern mommyhood, a Honda Pilot with Cheerios everywhere, everything a little sticky, trash stuck beneath the seats. "I need to clean this out," she'd explained, tossing her bag of running gear aside, shoes, mostly, as we'd loaded the car with posters. I'd been hired as a medical publications manager in gastroenterology because I had experience managing the publications of the results of clinical trials and post hoc analyses and health outcomes research for another pharmaceutical company, though this part, the part where we hung up scientific posters at conferences, or attended them at all, was new to me. The irony was that I'd only worked in publications for a little while, at a Danish company nearby. I found out how much they'd valued that experience when I met someone they'd hired for a similar position, later, on the neurology side of the business, who'd interviewed for my job, too.

But they had wanted me. It felt good, somehow, to feel

wanted, and my salary was $128,000 to start, base, with both short- and long-term bonuses that would make my total compensation jump to just shy of $162,000 a year. A friend told me to ask for more, so I asked for more, and got it, a couple thousand more a year from their original offer. I had no idea why I was being paid this much. I'd made $60 an hour at the Danish company, no benefits, via a temp agency who was surely charging the company at least $90 an hour to have me, and this, to me, was also a ridiculous sum of money. In graduate school, and before, my income had largely been somewhere in the $15,000 to $30,000 a year range. Working in the ER, I had cleared somewhere between $1,400 and $1,800 a month. My husband made about $50,000. I felt like this was some kind of wild, stupid game, like I had somehow conned an entire company into hiring me when I'd have worked for much less. And yet I knew people at the company or on the health-care advertising agency side of the business who made $250,000, or $400,000, or whatever. They bought million-dollar houses, went on exclusive Disney cruises, wanted to bend my ear over lunch so we could talk about the opportunities and tax advantages that lay in owning rental real estate. I caught the posters so they didn't slide out the back of Christine's SUV when she opened the hatch.

During my interview, she was so enthusiastic, I couldn't help but agree.

Yes, I'd love to work on just one compound.

Yes, I'd love to travel.

Yes, I'd love to develop relationships with *key opinion leaders*.

Yes, I am passionate about GI and the future of immunology.

Yes, I would learn the science. Of course.

And the first week, there was: Yes, I'd love to go to Zurich. Our company had offices there and they invited the Americans— me and my new boss—to attend a daylong meeting devoted to global medical publications for the compound on which I'd come to work.

My passport contained two stamps at that point, both from summers in Vilnius, Lithuania, as part of a writing workshop. I had never been anywhere else, except for a few hours in Toronto once in 2006, and then again, later, for my husband's cousins' weddings and his grandmother's funeral.

Yes, I said. I'd love to go to Zurich. There was just one issue: I had not yet been awarded a corporate American Express card, so I couldn't book a ticket.

Would you? my new boss asked. Could you put it on your personal card and then the company would reimburse you? You wouldn't have to carry a balance or anything.

Sure, I said. But the ticket cost $8,000. I wondered in what world I'd be offered $8,000 of credit. And it wasn't really $8,000. It was more like $11,000, after taxes and fees and the hotel in Zurich, a Marriott next door to the office. I'd never flown business class before.

I could get a coach seat, I said. That'd only run maybe $1,500, I thought, adding the math in my head.

My new boss laughed. Oh, *no*, she said, smiling. We can't have that. We'll just see if they can express the card.

✧ ✧ ✧

By the time the conference rolled around, I'd been working at the Japanese company six months but was still trying to get used to the way things were done. I'd leapt from my last job into this one, because I still needed the money. It was like this, somehow. Immediately after graduating from a writing program into nearly $70,000 in student debt, plus the medical debt that had not yet been forgiven, plus the new debts associated with our house and its repair, I had started working at the Danish company. I had told them I would do anything, yes, yes, yes, in the interview, and so they gave me the job, which would expand in scope and size over the following year and a half until I just couldn't take it anymore and quit and took all my anxiety and dread to my new job, at the Japanese company, a place I would also burn out from in the eighteen months that followed. I am aware that there are other ways of working, but I am simply not capable of them, as much as I've tried. I started as a project manager and then suddenly I was doing medical writing and then also managing the vendor for the medical writing, and then I was writing the annual report and releasing a quarterly publications newsletter and also managing a budget and planning the annual meeting for the department, as my boss became pregnant with twins, went on bed rest, and began micromanaging me from bed. But I had escaped that now. Fresh start. New job. I would know what my responsibilities were.

My husband says I have the opposite of white coat syndrome. I have a tendency to say yes to doctors, to science, because I want to be liked, in a way that makes sense to me at the time. It is the part of my personality that I would cut from my body and leave by the side of the road in an instant, no questions asked. I am socialized female, and so my body and my desires are mostly used as a shorthand for one or the other. I feel like I am supposed to say yes to everything. And mostly I do. I say yes to the work someone else was previously taking on. Yes to the thing I need to do. Yes to the thing I will do but have not completed yet. Yes to the work that is not mine. Yes to work that becomes mine. I am a string of yesses all the time, yes, yes, yes. I have never said no to my parents. It's good for temp jobs that I take and bad for careers I happen into, because invariably I end up doing work I hate. I had said yes to Julie for all of those

years, and now I would say yes to Christine and another boss
and everyone else.

✧ ✧ ✧

Just outside the conference hall at McCormick Place, everyone
wore suits, lanyards with badges, ribbons beneath indicating if
they were a first-time attendee or an old pro. The company I was
working for had won the right to print their name on the lan-
yard, which was big news, revealed at a meeting a couple weeks
before. Up until this point, I'd mostly attended writing conferences much less formal than this. At those events, we were less
like an academic conference and more like maybe Comic-Con,
with half the costumes, a lot of ripped jeans and T-shirts. It was
not unusual to get drunk at the writing conference on the floor
of the book fair, or see people have sex with strangers in the
hotel hallways late at night. But not here.

I was in Chicago for Digestive Disease Week, the world's
largest GI conference, a weeklong celebration of new research
and developments in gastroenterology, hepatology, GI surgery,
and endoscopy. It was supposed to be exciting, but mostly it was
terrible. I was still getting used to the idea of working on a single
compound, just one drug. At my previous pharma job, working
for the Danish company, I'd been responsible for a portfolio of
fourteen medications across several therapeutic areas, mostly
neurology and psychiatry. What this mostly meant is that I
didn't travel much. It was nice to stay home, to not have to focus
all my efforts on individual conferences. To play the part of the
project manager. I was good at that, the project management.
Now I was expected to attend all the conferences, to obtain
competitive intelligence on other drugs, to photograph posters,
to figure out how to draft a meta-analysis that would give our

compound an edge over the others at a subsequent conference. Spy versus spy. I didn't understand any of the science, but they were giving me time to catch up, to read everything I needed to learn about immunology, gastroenterology, how these types of drugs worked. Or they had, and now expected me to be ready to go. At these conferences, I'd have to meet the key opinion leaders and develop relationships with them, since they were doing research with our company. Like Dr. Desai.

Dr. Desai appeared like a mirage. There are certain kinds of specialties that you expect to dress or behave a particular way. Orthopods are attractive, nicely dressed jocks. ER docs are adrenaline junkies; a surprising number own fancy bikes, if they're not burned out, or maybe they scuba dive, or rock climb. Psychiatrists are crazy and wear a lot of chunky necklaces and flowy sweaters and skirts. But gastroenterologists are a specific kind of nerd. You can tell immediately if they are a surgery type or a procedure type. The procedure types are all neatly dressed, maybe a little boring, sweaters, jackets, ties, starched shirts that have gone a little limp. Across the conference floor, you could spot hundreds of heads with male-pattern baldness, like a sea of turtles. Surgery types are glossier, more aggressive. But Dr. Desai, a procedure type, was none of these things. He was a sharp dresser, attractive, with practical but good-looking shoes. He had good, thick black hair, wavy and cut well. He was collegial and charming and sort of alarmingly tall, maybe six-three, which made everything feel even more striking. He'd made my life a living hell for the past six months, and now I got to meet him. I extended my hand and smiled. "Hello! So great to finally meet in person," I said. My knees hurt and I was wearing black slacks and a sort of chunky-heeled shoe that I should've known how to describe but didn't. I got them on clearance, having sort of learned some basic tips on how to dress myself from a personal shopper at Nordstrom. I had succeeded in some ways and failed in others. The shoes were Cole Haan and made my feet bleed. I wore the lipstick the counter girl picked out for me when I got married. I just had the one color. I wasn't really into any of this. If left to my own devices, I'd stay home, or make friends with animals, not people. I couldn't stop smiling.

The conference floor looked like something had vomited on it. It was funny, almost, the idea that the conference floor had been changed for specifically this purpose. But the truth was, all these floors looked the same. When I thought about it later, I couldn't remember the difference between this conference or any of the others. It didn't help that a lot were held in the same locations. Chicago, DC, Vegas, Orlando. For the international conferences, maybe Vienna, a city I frequently referred to as the Pittsburgh of Europe, because it was full of a mix of brutalist architecture and gothic buildings, and because it was so gray in the winter.

There was the time in Vegas when the posters got lost in the mail and I had to reprint them at the nearest twenty-four-hour FedEx Kinkos at the cost of hundreds of dollars, a last-minute rush job. Or the time when some presenter failed to show up at his poster altogether, and we had to pull in someone else to present. It was boring, almost, the way the machine went. Everyone hired an agency to make these posters and the publications that would follow, which were supposed to be just interesting enough to get people to read them, because the information on them was usually not that important. Such was the problem of publishing old data. Most of what I worked on were old data. The primary analyses had already been done, and now here we were, looking at the future, scraping the bottom of the barrel. The drug in question, an IV infusion of an immunology drug meant to treat Crohn's disease and ulcerative colitis, was supposed to be a great drug. It'd been a great success for the company, a billion-dollar drug. That was what they called it, a special category by itself. A billion dollars. The first billion-dollar drug was Tagamet. Now billion-dollar drugs—where the revenue for the drug exceeds a billion dollars—are commonplace. Retail, the drug I worked on cost about $50,000 to $60,000 a year, per patient. When I interviewed for this job, I told them I'd be happy to learn a new therapeutic area, to understand the workings of the gut and the immunology that mediated it. But I lied. I was hoping the new science would come via osmosis. I'd learned so much of the science at the old company because of my interest in the brain and how I'd taken twenty-six drugs over five years. The new science—the GI science—was a different world altogether. And the publications budget, which I oversaw, was a drop in the bucket compared to everything else, about $1.4 million a year.

And, in the days leading up to Digestive Disease Week, Dr. Desai wouldn't stop texting me. He wanted to know if he could fly business class, because he didn't want to fly coach. No, I would explain, we had a policy that he couldn't fly business on flights lasting less than four hours. Or maybe it was six hours. In any case, we were not giving him a business-class flight. Other companies did this, bent the rules, or had different rules. We were known for being the conservative company, with specific expectations around physician reimbursement. The Sunshine Act, the product of a bipartisan push among senators to regulate physician reimbursement in the pharmaceutical industry, had been implemented just a few years ago, and everyone had a different idea of what to do and how to follow it. The Sunshine Act told us that we had to declare how we reimbursed physicians for research, for advisory boards. Gone were the days where someone in the pharmaceutical industry could buy someone a swimming pool for giving a talk, or so some folks had heard. Pharma had deep pockets, but there were rules now. Like not giving business-class flights to people who were sitting in a plane seat for less than four hours.

Still, he texted me all the time. Because he was from an institution on the West Coast, his day ended later than mine. I came in at seven, tried to be done by four. But that never worked: he'd call or text at four-thirty or five and sounded disappointed if I wasn't there to answer his text or call. If I didn't immediately respond, he'd call the medical director I dotted-line reported to, a lifer, a woman who believed fiercely in the work she did and didn't have much space for anything else. She had brought this drug to the market, and its predecessor, and would be there for the drugs that followed. She knew everything there was to know about the billion-dollar drug, its history, safety, efficacy, and every single study ever made. Recently, she had appeared on a panel about work-life balance and women at the company and confessed to the room that she recently tried to pick up her son at his school and they wouldn't let him go with her because they didn't know who she was. The woman who actually reported to her, a PhD with two kids, would send her an emoji at the end of the night to let her know she was going to bed and no longer available to respond to her texts or emails, which started up again many mornings at five a.m.

✧ ✧ ✧

The goal had been to quit my job at the Danish company, to pay off my debts and just never return. I had stopped sleeping; my heart started racing in bed. I was burned out and sick and tired and kept getting diagnosed with additional autoimmune diseases. The original plan was to work for a few months, maybe a year, then live small as we had in grad school and before so I could spend the time writing my book, but then we bought this dilapidated apartment building with three units, and the scope of the work kept expanding, and I never seemed to get any closer to paying off over $70,000 in student loans. It seemed like an impossible figure, the $70,000, but it was compounded by the $33,000 in new furnaces and duct work and air conditioning, which my husband insisted we didn't need but I got talked into doing, the $40,000 we ended up paying my brother, the tens of thousands we had to pay someone else to fix the work my brother had left unfinished, and my medical debt, which never went away. I was making good money, but everything I made went to the house, to finish the building, or toward our consumer or my medical debt, which also loomed large on the horizon. We'd bought the building from the bank in a foreclosure sale, and it hadn't been well constructed. There were past termites, present termites, socks in the walls as insulation, sweaters and plastic bags wrapped around leaky pipes, and the back half of the building was actively falling off. Several drains were not connected to any kind of sewer system and drained into the backyard instead. My dad kept coming over while we were at our jobs and ordering guys to expand the scope of the work, then would push me for a check at the end of the day. My brother, too, would tear up floors or scrap ducts or do whatever he wanted during the day, under the guise of helping me with our building. We'd have to pay him, or someone else, to fix these things. So I kept working.

The competitive intelligence part was hard for outsiders to understand. In order to be effective, you had to know the history of publishing these posters at conferences, whether they were yours or from another company. We prided ourselves on being more conservative than other companies when it came to slicing data, but this mostly just made it more difficult to compare our data with theirs. Our competitors did things like tell us that their drug started working in just a few days. That was the latest thing—to have a drug that showed efficacy in just two weeks, or less. This was a sort of impossible scenario. None of the original studies had really demonstrated this kind of efficacy, for our drug or for anyone else's. Instead, we'd slice the data to look at other markers for efficacy, to essentially use a meta-analysis to explain to these key opinion leaders at the conference that our drug could see results in just two weeks. Or else, compared to old drug treatments, the new stuff worked faster and had fewer complications. My life was a lot of Kaplan-Meier survival curves then: How long until someone had a complication? What interventions made those complications less likely? We're slicing data so fine that the ns just get smaller and smaller with each pass. Everyone does it: n is the number of patients in the study, and with these sub-analyses, we could find ns of fifteen, or seven, or five. I had taken enough statistics classes to know that there is little value you can derive from five patients.

✧ ✧ ✧

Mostly, for me, work meant wandering around the conference and snapping photos of competitor posters with similarly small ns and attempting to glad-hand people when necessary. Like Dr. Desai. He was allegedly working on some real-world results using our drug and others in a head-to-head study, so the relationship was considered incredibly valuable. We had done something along the lines of offering free drugs to him and his study. We'd supported the publication of results through fancy posters at conferences like these. And we'd paid his airfare to come to the conference, put him up in a nice hotel, paid for meals. Some doctors had relationships with their hospitals that forbade these kinds of interactions, or limited them, so we'd have to be careful. The key in all of this was the concept of transfer of value—a way to explain how we provided value to a physician or health-care provider. Maybe that transfer of value came in posters and publications or hotel stays, or maybe it came in something else. In any case, the biggest issue was that our company listed these sorts of publication benefits—printing posters, editing posters—as a transfer of value, a reportable expense to the federal government, and our competitors didn't.

✧ ✧ ✧

On the conference floor, each day, you could see dozens of physicians lining up at each booth, getting their badges scanned to indicate they got a free coffee. One booth offered free tacos; another one, hamburger sliders. Our booth was coffee only, espresso, Americano, that sort of thing. Not sure about cappuccino. I can't remember now if we drew the line at foamed milk. We didn't want to be like these other people who offered more. But it seemed like it hardly mattered, they were all offering more. One exhibit provided cotton candy and a model mini Ferris wheel, the drug name printed on each basket. At another, you could watch physicians play miniature golf as the pharma rep detailed them on the latest in opioid-induced constipation treatments. It had many holes, color-coded balls, and an enormous lawn in Astroturf, unfurled and stapled to the framed-out hills and trees and shrubs that made up this bizarro landscape. Where they lined up to play, the docs watched the national commercial for the drug. There were prizes for the winners, though I didn't stop to ask what they were. When I swung by to surreptitiously take photos of the exhibit, I flipped my badge around so I wasn't there on official work business and got a strange look from one of the reps, who assumed I was there for competitive intelligence purposes. I wasn't. I was just there because it was the most ridiculous thing I'd ever seen.

✧ ✧ ✧

When they bring it back the following year, at the next Digestive Disease Week, beginning of June, all the holes, the fake forest, the orange-and-white banner proclaiming that it is *the new choice for opioid-induced constipation*, this terrifying diorama, I know I have to quit this job. It's not enough to work for the company that serves only coffee at events like these. Is the science from Dr. Desai's group interesting? Valuable? Absolutely—we have no idea how our drug behaves in the real world. But we are performing all of this at an expense that's hard to bear. Yes, the research everyone does is important. Yes, the work to take a drug from preclinical stages to the market is huge and hugely expensive. But the rest—the advertising, the television com-mercials, the hamburger sliders, the endless catered lunches, the agency money, the plane tickets to Europe—are all, directly or not, contributing to this enormous cost. We are working on a publication, Dr. Desai and I, one that will end up in a well-regarded medical journal, no doubt. He's been writing it himself to avoid transfer of value concerns with his institution, though he's also told me that other companies don't report transfer of value in this way, and that in his contract with a different phar-maceutical company, he can send all of this to the health-care agency instead. In the meantime, I've kept a Post-it note on my desk over the course of the last year, detailing what I owe and to whom. Every few days, I log into one of my many online accounts to make an electronic payment. It's excruciating. I'm so burned out I can't make sense of my days anymore—once back from the conference, I just stare at spreadsheets and try to avoid my email, until I get the one about my short-term bonus for the year, something that's awarded in mid-June provided you stay that long. It's $22,864, an astonishing sum, enough to pay off the rest of my student loans, the last bit of all this garbage, so I walk into my boss's office to tell her I quit.

Something for
the Pain

The air freshener at the Cosmopolitan felt like a middle-school dance: a crush of Axe body spray and sweat. There were low lights beneath fabric swags; strings of crystal draped from the ceiling. The floor sparkled, opulent, and the casino hummed dark inside. Every wall and piece of furniture was decorated in purple, gray, or black, like a nightclub, or a bruise.

Las Vegas felt a little too on the nose for a pain conference, but here we were: over two thousand frontline practitioners gathered together for PAINWeek 2019, the largest medical conference in the country devoted to this specific genre of suffering, held at the Cosmopolitan for ten years running. Outside, it was September on the Strip, hot enough to melt your sandals to the sidewalk. Inside, the hotel heavily advertised a show titled *Opium*; there were brochures and discounted tickets, and I'd seen billboards up and down the Strip. Attendees walked past the booth selling tickets on the way to the conference rooms each morning, and I wanted to stop and talk to someone about it, just because of the name, but I couldn't imagine what I'd say.

I was here because I'd heard that chronic pain patients across the country were being denied their medication. Ever since the CDC had issued guidelines in August 2018 indicating the upper limit of 90 milligram morphine equivalents (MMEs) per day, the pain community had been in uproar. Most pain medicine health-care providers found this limit concerning; they often saw patients who were stable on much higher doses or even double this number, yet with the implementation of the new guideline, many practitioners felt forced to taper their patients down to a smaller dose or off opioids altogether. Opioids and health-care providers who prescribe them have been unfairly demonized, they claimed. Opioids were just one of several tools health-care providers used for pain management, but many of the others had become less popular or weren't covered by insurance. The problem of possible opioid abuse, always top of mind, was managed in a variety of ways: at the conference, there were sessions on abuse-deterrent drugs, sessions on alternative medicine, information on drug dosing, a panel on urine drug screening for pain patients, and a lot in between. Basically, if your patients were abusing drugs, there were plenty of strategies on how to deter them, treat their pain, and still retain your medical license in the process.

In the Brera Ballroom that first morning, breakfast consisted of a fruit smoothie, a breakfast burrito, coffee, orange juice, pastries. The program—Managing Chronic Pain with Abuse-Deterrent Extended-Release Opioids: Clinical Evidence and Implications, sponsored by Collegium Pharmaceutical—was scheduled for eight-thirty a.m. At the door, representatives from Collegium had scanned our badges so the transfer of value associated with this breakfast could be reported in accordance with the Sunshine Act. These types of programs were a mainstay of medical conferences: a "key opinion leader," generally a physician or physician assistant, or nurse practitioner with a lot of influence, talking about the latest and greatest in better living through chemistry. Over breakfast burritos and soggy pastries, you took in a series of slides with pharmacokinetic data, maybe a phase 4 study, some safety profiles. That morning's program covered a drug called Xtampza. The main discussion at many of these breakfasts at PAINWeek was around abuse-deterrent opioids, drugs that became less effective if you crushed and snorted them or injected them or took them in any way other than the way they had been prescribed. This path of deterrence had become popular among pharmaceutical companies as a way to hedge against the opioid crisis; the first reformulation for OxyContin occurred in 2010, when Purdue Pharma made the drug harder to abuse. What wasn't described during our sponsored breakfast, but mentioned in several panels later, was the spike in heroin use following the release of the abuse-deterrent formulation.

The Brera Ballroom felt like every other conference meal I'd ever attended: too fancy for regular dining, but not quite a wedding. The room was scattered with eight-feet-round tables, each with a place setting and too many glasses; along one wall, ostensibly the front, there was a podium and a series of drop-down screens for the slide presentation that would follow. Our table, at one corner of the room, included a physician assistant with the Indian Health Service in New Mexico, a middle-aged woman physician who worked in a pain clinic in Upstate New York, an East Indian couple from Texas. The PA talked about how fentanyl was big where he lived, that it was mostly cut with honey, that it all was coming in from China lately. The other big thing his patients used for pain was peyote—but that's *spiritual*, he emphasized, so he couldn't touch that. I didn't ask him what he meant.

Brandy, the pain clinic physician from Upstate New York, leaned over and whispered, "I put everyone on this. It's a great drug."

"Oh yeah?" I said. I hadn't told anyone that I was there in a journalistic capacity. I had registered as an EMT, which is what I used to do. Most everyone was there for the continuing medical education (CME) credits: there were a lot, and the conference squeezed credits in at every available opportunity. A woman scanned my badge when I got into the breakfast, thinking that they would total my CME attendance at the end of the conference and give me a certificate so I could renew my nonexistent medical license. It's not exactly lying, I told myself. I was an EMT once.

"I don't tell them it's an abuse-deterrent compound, just that it's new, and *safer*," Brandy said.

Safer is a code word among the opioid-patient population. In online forums, these patients trade secrets on how to get the medication they say they need: which pain clinics will see them, who prescribes what, who's been cut off or forcibly tapered. So many of these patients had been cut off, they resorted to creative ways to find relief. Maybe they'd take kratom, a plant from Southeast Asia with psychotropic properties popular among the pain community, which was not technically illegal. Or they'd try to switch pain clinics, or maybe they would reserve their medication for when they needed it most, as a way to increase the individual dose. There were muscle relaxants, prescription-strength NSAIDs. A few admitted to obtaining fentanyl or heroin, but the conversation was about pain rather than addiction. "Dependent, but not addicted" remains the constant refrain in groups like these. The fear that the pain may return is enough to keep patients doing whatever they can to stay above the pain line. Everyone is concerned about what happens when they have pain between doses, maybe due to a dosing failure, or maybe because it's just not cutting it anymore—what the medical community calls "breakthrough pain." There are different types: dosing failure—when doses come at the wrong time and aren't able to get patients to the next dose without pain; predictable incidents—same activity yields the same pain; unpredictable pain—when patients performing the same activities have new pain; and the worst—idiopathic pain, or new pain with no known cause or reason.

There's a fine line between a pain patient and a drug addict, and sometimes patients go back and forth across it. This is what we were effectively discussing that morning and throughout the conference.

From working in the ER, I know patients lie. I think of Kathleen, my friend, my coworker in the ER. She went to rehab for heroin, relapsed, and is stable on methadone, last I checked. What health-care providers are supposed to do about this problem depends on who you ask. It seems important to be suspicious of patient intentions, even if they tell you the truth.

According to the course objectives that morning, we were there to "discuss key issues surrounding the opioid epidemic and consequences of opioid diversion, misuse, and abuse"; to "review the clinical profile and data supporting an abuse-deterrent opioid option"; and to "explore flexible administration options." Everything is code for something else; breakfast was really a presentation on a particular drug that was newer to the market, a review of their data. Diversion—when patients sell or divert their prescription drugs from medical to nonmedical or illicit use—was a big part of the discussion. Sometimes patients stick with the same drugs; sometimes they trade up to something stronger, or just something new. Diversion happens in a lot of different ways: through patients selling their own prescriptions, certainly, but some people believe that diversion happens when patients stop taking their drugs as prescribed and start crushing and snorting them instead, or injecting them, or taking too many at a time. Any treatment feels dangerous with these patients, according to the health-care providers who treat them, like pain patients could all ride off the rails at any moment and crash into a lifetime of drug addiction and dependence, and eventually, with some patients, an overdose, and maybe death.

At the end, the presenter took questions. This drug is formulated to be less effective if you crush and snort or inject it: the bioavailability stays the same. Nobody had any questions. Most of the table had experience with the drug and came mainly for breakfast.

In the hallway, I thought I glimpsed someone I knew from my pharma days, but knew this couldn't have been the case; he was a gastroenterologist, not a pain-medicine guy. Still, it was disorienting. I kept getting caught by this sort of dilemma. I found myself standing in line for the exhibitors/industry people rather than the attendee line for registration, where I belonged. Before I quit, I worked for a multinational pharmaceutical company, attending conferences like this one. At those companies, I'd manage the publication of scientific posters for their presentations. We would present new or old data at conferences like these (the old data was labeled "encore presentations"), and it was my job to manage a team of medical writers who published the results of clinical trials and health outcomes research. I was not very good at it; routinely, our agency would not deliver the posters in time or they'd have errors that I'd missed, and I'd have to scramble over to a FedEx in the middle of the night to reprint them. I spent the rest of my time at these conferences wandering around and trying to understand competitors' posters, so we could present some sliver of data in a new way at the next conference. There was a part of me, however erroneous, that believed I was at PAINWeek to hang posters and make sure key opinion leaders showed up in front of them.

Flipping through the conference app, nearly all the sessions had cheeky titles: Icebergs, Oceans, and the Experience of

Pain; The Gang That Couldn't Shoot Straight: Reconsidering the CDC Guideline; I'm Not a Doctor, but I Play One in DC. I tried to select the content that seemed relevant to my query— programming about policy, about how frontline practitioners are expected to treat patients. At the CDC guideline panel, the room was packed: everyone wanted to hear from Dr. Gary Jay, who was discussing the CDC guideline for opioid prescribing and its failures, of which the room believed were many. Jay is a neurologist and a professor of medicine at UNC–Chapel Hill.

Pain docs feel they're being treated unfairly. Yes, there were bad actors, but not as many as described. Yes, there are pill mills, but most of them have been shut down. In the meantime, the government is interfering with physicians and other health-care practitioners' ability to do their jobs. The government should not be regulating how many MMEs you prescribe; it just creates more paperwork, results in more prescriptions for the same drugs. There had been a lot of discussion around the fact that the United States writes a lot more prescriptions for opioid medications than Canada. What many don't realize is that a lot of physicians can no longer write for more than a few pills at a time because of new state legislation; to get around this, they write more prescriptions. In Canada, you could write one prescription for X number of pills and three refills; in the United States, that equaled at least four prescriptions, and possibly more, depending on the dosing. In Florida alone, you are not allowed to write more than three days' worth at a time, meaning Florida physicians are stuck writing hundreds of prescriptions for their chronic pain patients. Dr. Jay explained that this sort of thing is representative of a larger problem that began in the late 1980s, when insurance companies stopped covering everything besides opioids. This is true: biofeedback, acupuncture, and other non-pharmaceutical pain management tools stopped being covered, resulting in more prescriptions. The opioid crisis didn't happen overnight; it was a slow, steady burn comprised of issues that seemed small and individual at the time and combined to make the difficult storm we see in the news each day.

When we talked later, the news was terrifying. Chronic pain patients were finding it nearly impossible to see anyone who could treat their condition. "There was a study done in Michigan that showed 41 percent of 189 practices would not take a patient who was taking an opioid. Forty-two percent would at least look at the patient, and 17 percent said give us some more information. But 41 percent wouldn't see the patient," Dr. Jay explained. A number of potential patients who wanted to see Dr. Jay instead completed suicide because they couldn't wait the time required to see him, or because their insurance denied them the option of seeing him, or because they couldn't get there. Whether you have cancer or chronic musculoskeletal pain, the likelihood of suicide due to chronic pain is at least doubled compared to the general population. Dr. Jay had a lot of stories like this. "I had a patient from another state who sent me an email and wanted to become a patient, and I told her, I need to see your records and your referrals and I'd be happy to see you. This was a chronic pain patient who'd been taken off her meds. And two weeks later, I found out she killed herself."

I originally tried writing this story starting with pain patients whom I connected with through Facebook groups or online bulletin boards. So many of them would speak to me for a while, then stop, and I'd find out later that they didn't make it, only because a relative would log on to their profile and let everyone know, maybe link to an obituary. Many more attempted suicide and then returned to the groups a few months later, their posts filled with heartbroken emojis. Periodically, a member of the community would "check in" with everyone to see how they were doing, ask them to respond with a colored-heart emoji: green meant good, black meant you needed help and didn't know where to turn. These kinds of discussions were not uncommon for patients with chronic pain.

I decided to attend all the sponsored breakfasts and lunches I could, because I wanted to be able to tell everyone what was really going on in the pharmaceutical industry. If a member of the public, outside the medical world, wants to know what legal drug pushing looks like, they should attend a sponsored break-fast. I never worked on the sales side in pharma, so I only knew part of what this resembled; I had heard of physicians demand-ing particular kinds of attention, like rock stars with compli-cated riders, but only knew of it secondhand until later in my pharma career. We called the people who lectured at sponsored breakfasts or dinners collectively "speakers bureaus," people who could be relied on to draw a crowd, folks who had the kind of natural charisma and pull to tell their fellow practitioners about the opportunities that would result from prescribing this drug over another one. It's almost a popularity contest: pharma companies vie for the practitioners who give the best speeches, those who draw the biggest crowds. There's something in that for the speakers, of course: some of them can make over a thou-sand bucks an hour, or more, by participating in this system. Physicians like Dr. Jay can't do it; his institution, UNC–Chapel Hill, prevents him from opting into agreements like these. Some institutions, like the University of Iowa Hospitals and Clinics, for example, won't even allow drug reps on their cam-pus. So those who consult for the pharmaceutical industry are a small, elite group, which means a lot of them consult for a lot of different pharmaceutical companies. This showed up in the first day's breakfast and also the second's: both speakers had long lists of disclosures, companies they'd consulted for. I quietly judged them for this ridiculous list that each of them rattled off while flashing a slide with the list on the screen.

I felt like I was unfairly critiquing the health-care industry at large. It's hard to explain, I told folks outside pharma. Yes, the pharmaceutical companies are trying to develop relationships with physicians and other health-care providers (nurse practitioners and physician assistants are especially popular, as they don't have to be paid as much as docs do). Yes, they make more money with an increase in prescriptions. But we also live in an atmosphere of choice, where there are thousands of drugs developed in the United States that are then marketed around the world. The money that the United States makes subsidizes drugs in other countries, particularly Europe, whose regulations prevent the sort of pricing that happens in the States. Ultimately, someone is paying for the cost of drug development, which includes salaries for its employees.

So what now? everyone kept saying. What do we do if our patients are abusing? At one panel on trauma and pain, the speaker, a middle-aged white guy and physician, told us that yes, their patients have pain, but they also have emotional pain, and emotions can amplify physical pain, that there have been studies. Other speakers skirted the issue, talking about how insurance companies will reimburse for more invasive procedures, like back surgery, but won't pay for acupuncture, physical therapy, or pain pills. One panel focused mostly on teaching patients better coping skills so they could learn to manage their pain more effectively, to learn to move, that a lot of chronic pain patients have kinesiophobia, or a fear of movement, which prevents them from moving and essentially worsens their pain, particularly among patients with arthritis, fibromyalgia, or other issues. Another panel was about finding better ways to manage urine drug screening, a mainstay among pain patients, though not every company has the screening procedures that might be most helpful. They told us that all providers should urine drug screen their patients with every visit, to see if their opioid use has expanded beyond the boundaries of what's been prescribed. I asked the woman next to me, a middle-aged family medicine physician from Maryland, if she drug tests her patients every time. "Of course," she said, giving me a look.

I attended the panel on fibromyalgia because my internist says I have it, among a host of other autoimmune issues (Hashimoto's, adult-onset asthma, endometriosis) I've inherited over the past ten years, plus TMJ, the panel I couldn't attend because it was too depressing (there is no cure, only management). When I worked in the pharma industry, I spent a lot of time on airplanes and at desks, solitary, without motion. I learned from the lecturer on fibromyalgia pain that this is a big part of what's perpetuated my own pain. Conferences were things to endure. Food was always questionable. Even sitting at this conference for a few days caused my body to seize up; I spent the evenings pacing the Strip in ninety-degree heat, but it wasn't enough. The lecturer, too, had fibromyalgia; she used her experience as a patient to help other patients like her. She talked about the rigorous exercise she did to stay healthy, how she spent evenings on the treadmill or the elliptical at the conference hotel. I've found that this idea—that providers are also patients—is not uncommon. The attendees of the panel were almost entirely women. I'm not on pain pills, but I occasionally take my husband's medical marijuana. There is the truth that my family history is rife with alcohol and drug abuse, so I need to be careful about what I use and when. Maybe the muscle relaxants I periodically take could lead to something stronger, but I've tried everything else: acupuncture, Chinese herbs, high

intensity interval training, which I eventually discovered is supposed to be bad for my Hashimoto's. I could ask my internist
for something more. This, too, feels like the wrong approach, a
dangerous bargain, a place I could slip off.

By Saturday, I found a panel where they told us that some
people are simply wired for abuse. We know this, of course,
because of the way that alcoholism and drug abuse carves a
line in families. What is especially surprising is that the gene
of abuse is not common, which gives credence to the idea that
most of these pain patients are "dependent, but not addicted."
This is part of what makes all of this complicated and hard for
the public to understand. That there are some patients who
take OxyContin or even fentanyl, a drug a hundred times more
powerful than morphine, and they remain stable on the same
dosage for years, even decades. Then there are others whose
drug needs exceed their practitioner's prescribing abilities,
who are cut off and turn to street drugs in between. That it's
hard to tell who is who in all of this.

As the panel concluded, two women who sat in front of me
turned to each other.

"Do you want to go get margaritas?" one asked.

"Ab-so-*lute*-ly," the other replied.

II.

Typically, when any patient arrives to their physician's office or
the ER, there are four vital signs: body temperature, blood pressure, pulse, and breathing rate. The fifth vital sign, pain, made
its way into public consciousness in the late nineties. Adopted
by the Veterans Health Administration in 1999, this fifth vital
sign was supposed to be incorporated into all patient encoun-
ters: Did the patient have pain, and if so, how severe was it? The
Joint Commission, which accredits hospital and care facilities

in the United States, followed the VHA's lead by adopting pain as the fifth vital sign in 2001, requiring every health-care provider to ask about pain in every encounter with patients. This request showed up in the ER and in doctors' offices: Are you in pain? What's the quality of your pain? Does it move anywhere? Can you rate your pain on a scale from zero to ten, zero being no pain and ten being the worst imaginable? These were the kinds of questions I'd ask as an EMT and ER tech, dozens of times a day. In the ER, I did this in intake so we could check it off before we did anything else. Unsurprisingly, nearly everyone we saw was in some kind of pain. Otherwise they wouldn't be in the ER.

Pain as a vital sign is not working and hasn't worked for a very long time, possibly ever, but we're still using it because that's what the Joint Commission has recommended. Now, every interaction on the software platform Epic, the largest electronic medical records system in the United States, prompts the clinician to ask if the patient is in pain. In my training as an EMT, I'd have to ask the patient if they were in pain as part of my checklist of things to do, after making sure I was wearing appropriate PPE and ascertaining that the patient had a patent airway, was breathing, and that their body was circulating blood the way it should.

So how did we get here?

✧ ✧ ✧

The ER is a great place to go if you are having a heart attack or stroke or if you are in an accident of some kind, though fewer patients are doing that anymore either, and the ones who do now have COVID on top of their traumatic injury or illness. Historically, if you can't stop vomiting or can't breathe, you're supposed to go to the ER. This is less true if you need something like Dilaudid, which is the sort of thing people used to come in for more frequently but can't anymore. If you came for pain, we just treated the pain where it was, then sent you off with a referral to your primary care physician. There were no pain clinic referrals at our ER, just "see your doctor," and that was it. The Dilaudid was incredibly effective but short-lived. Patients would come in, say they wanted the *D* drug, what was it called? No, we'd have to say. No, no, no. We'd dispense muscle relaxants, maybe ibuprofen or acetaminophen if we were concerned about drug dependency, and then you would be on your way.

We'd see patients who needed something and weren't honest about why: a woman with intractable pain. She knew our doctors, our people, who worked when, like Kathleen did. We made a note on her file for drug-seeking behavior, then offered her acetaminophen and nothing else, a discharge note, a suggestion she look at different options for pain management. We didn't explain what those options might entail, or how she might find a way to manage her suffering now, in the moment. She cursed at us, maybe threw something. I remember hiding in the break room with the PA who treated her, saying that we just had to stay here for a little longer, that she'd leave, and if not, security would be called. I think of her often now, wonder if she's still alive, what we did, how we failed her and most everyone else. If she's on the message boards or on Facebook, earthbound, bodybound, posting photos of her dog or maybe a cat—I think of her as having a pet—still unable to leave the house.

III.

Lately, on Facebook, the chronic pain patient groups and my friends' timelines have started to look the same. I joined all these groups because I wanted to understand what chronic pain patients did with their time, especially during lockdown, how they passed the hours. The ways in which they tried to beat the clock, knowing that they only had to get by long enough to take the next dose. Dependent, but not addicted. The porches of dosing are slung between acres of arid landscape, and we are drifting through. Everyone trying to get to the next meal, the next Zoom meeting, the next pocket of time away from their kids, away from family. Time stopped but also stretched.

I barely show up for anything in person anymore. I have half a dozen autoimmune diseases, most of which put my body in some kind of chronic pain.

When I develop another weird, painful rash on my body, or wake up some mornings and my elbows don't work, I take blurry photos and send them to my internist, who says he doesn't know what the rashes are, but maybe they're ringworm? I have not spent any time in locker rooms. It is not ringworm.

I tell people I'll mail them weed through the US Pot Service instead. My husband has had a medical marijuana card in Illinois for a long time, and he gets access to all the good stuff. There is a woman named Mindy who won a James Beard Award and makes fantastic edibles here in Chicago. She is the good stuff, we tell people, because she is. I am taking them because they put a dent in what I seem to feel every day. It's just a dent, or maybe a suggestion of a dent. I never thought of myself as someone who would use this to get through.

❖ ❖ ❖

We are preparing for something, but we don't know what that is. When things will shift. The unknowing of it makes it impossible to plan for, to make sense of. There is the low current of anxiety that curls through everything. I bought grow lights and am growing herbs and microgreens in the house, but I'm thinking of growing weed instead.

When I used to work in the ER, we could help only a small fraction of the folks who came in. I think about that a lot now, as the COVID cases rise, as people drop dead in ERs, or more likely, after feeling better for a week on a ventilator, get disconnected and then suddenly stop living. No one was prepared for this, neither doctors nor anyone else. In medical training, it's the sick kids who compensate and then dive off the edge of a cliff, not the adults. Adults are supposed to make slow, measurable progress toward death, or else recover slowly. The general public doesn't know this, or that emergency is not really all emergencies and probably not your emergency. Many people can't be helped. We'd see the same people all the time, women with the kinds of autoimmune diseases I have now, people with chronic pain whose issues we could never resolve.

I try to sign up for an LSD microdosing trial, only to find out I live too far away. Ketamine is now FDA approved, but I won't qualify: it's only for the most intractable of depressions. I still wash my hair, which is probably worth something in all of this. It has gotten very long. At a friend's barn, I ride other people's horses, casting circles slowly around the ring, watching hoofprints in the sand. It's a distraction from the reality of my body, which comes into sharp focus whenever I get off the horse and brush him and put him back in his field with his friends. The horse I'm riding is sometimes lame, takes a wrong step here or there. His owner is trying to figure out what is wrong with him. Is what I'm doing drug-seeking behavior? Hard to say.

With the news that Purdue Pharma is being disbanded, some of the chronic pain patients are increasingly worried about access to OxyContin, despite the fact that the drugmaker is continuing to make it, just in a nonprofit capacity, with any profits diverted to drug management and recovery programs. The federal government is now, essentially, in the business of manufacturing opiates. Some pain patients are suspicious that their pain medication will be limited more, that soon the DEA will touch everything. There are other opioid manufacturers. It could be worse. A writer friend thinks that there will be shortages and is trying to ration her doses accordingly.

I am always suspect of people in pain. Or I was. Or I can be. I think of these dusty porches of dosing when I'm counting out ibuprofen. It doesn't do anything, the ibuprofen, except maybe give me ulcers, but I like to think it does.

I wonder what everyone in the pain groups are up to. How do they manage? How do they cope? They're still there, these people, pandemic layered over pandemic like sediment. I want to know what's happening a few layers down. In one group, they have put the suicide hotline in the header, so people can have someone to call. Several people in the online group have been offered ketamine or Haldol in the ER to manage their pain, though it doesn't work. Another asks why his urine drug screen is showing up with a drug he doesn't take; another member suggests that kratom can cause a false positive.

✦ ✦ ✦

At my doctor's office for a masked annual physical, my internist depression screens me. I know it's because Epic, the online medical record system he uses, prompts him to do so. Northwestern Medicine is part of a program that uses an installation of Epic that depression screens everyone.

There are a series of questions, mostly yes/no: Have I had any feelings of sadness in the last two weeks? Do I have any thoughts of self-harm? What about thoughts of hurting others? he asks. I tell him that if anyone says they're fine right now, that should trigger a depression screen follow-up. He laughs. I laugh. He tries to ask another question. "It's like choose your own adventure," I tell him, waving him off. Just pick something and move on. Everyone knows that physical pain and mental pain are linked, but they haven't known this always. I want to ask my doctor what he knows about this link, except that he doesn't really know. We are limited here, still. He clicks something on the screen. We move on.

After

Years from now, Julie will come to me in a dream. We will be on a bus together, going somewhere, or nowhere, or maybe in a streetcar around Pittsburgh, even though they took the streetcars out in the seventies. I am not crazy, I'll tell her. She will sit close to me, reclined. A child will approach us and tell me a secret, though I can't make out what he's saying. Then, suddenly, we will appear inside a large white room that holds a sink but is not a bathroom, a room that reminds me of the examination room of one of my hospitalizations. Where she conducted a physical on me once. Funny, a physical by a psychiatrist on a mental patient. Then we will wash our hands together. This is a good idea, I say. Then I repeat that I'm not crazy, that I never was, just lonely, confused, depressed a little, maybe, but not insane. She will look up and turn to me.

You are, she will say. You didn't sleep enough and you had ridiculous ideas of what you thought was normal.

But normal is not real, and neither is the dream. In truth I avoid Iowa City altogether now because I fear running into her on the street all these years later, maybe at the strip-mall Dairy Queen close to her new office, or at the other one, closest to where she and her new husband have bought a house, a low-slung ranch, for her aging parents, to keep them nearby. I want to go back when I'm ready, when I've made something of myself, to tell her, here, I turned out okay after all. Not crazy, I want to tell her, even though I know all this stuff about her. Normal, happy, survived that dark time in my life. My medical life is less complex now. Instead of monthly or even weekly trips to a psychiatrist, I go once a year to check my thyroid levels, my vitamin D deficiency. I've worked with a speech pathologist to learn the unwritten social rules of turn-taking and speech patterns and how to give signals that indicate I am listening to what others say. All those years of sleep distur- bances and weirdness boiled down to hormones and neuro- logical difference.

But the truth is, I don't know the truth. Don't know if maybe I could have been crazy and just resistant to all those drugs she prescribed, that in trying to design a life for myself I missed out on or forgot about the times when the drugs might have worked. There were differences in my behavior at times—and I could have or can attribute those to certain drugs, maybe. But I could just as easily attribute them to other things—some strange hormones, or whether I had exercised or eaten or had human interaction that day. In a sense, all of those hundreds of visits and hundreds of pages of records I requested again and again—trying to make sense of the person I was at the time— may or may not mean anything at all.

And maybe that's the difficulty in writing this or any other life—that in making sense of what I've done or seen or said, I'm trying to rationalize, trying to order away those parts of my life that felt absolutely unordered, strange, or nonsensical.

And so I try to parse out the anxiety of what to say. If I was crazy, and if so, for how long. How things—like the dream I had—didn't make sense then, but still, in the internal logic of that dream, Julie knew there was something wrong with me, something clinical.

So dream me watches her wash her hands, watches the bubbles slide over her pale pink manicure, the new rings on her left hand, curly hair falling over one shoulder. You need to take something, dream Julie says. She rinses her hands beneath the faucet, and I watch the water puddle in the sink, then slip down the drain. She wants to tell me something else, too. But then I wake up, and as it turns out, I'm okay.

Acknowledgments

There were so many people who helped me with this book, long before it was a book.

Matt McGowan, for your belief in and support of my work and my career and for being the calm, rational voice of reason in all of this madness.

MacDowell, thank you for your incredibly generous support when I needed it most. I cannot express this enough. Also many thanks to VCCA and SLS-Lithuania.

For the staff at Dollop/Hoosier Mama Pie Company, where I rewrote most of this book from the early morning until you guys started cooking onions every day. For my fellow groomers at PetSmart & fellow ER techs.

Paul Reyes and Allison Wright, for your expert guidance and faith in my strangeness. Jim Hamblin, for accepting a very early piece from this manuscript many years ago. Leslie Jamison, for your support of my work, particularly in selecting "Cost of Living" for *Best American Essays*.

Rose Andersen, for potato feelings, always. Erin Khar for countless Zoom dates. Monica Kass Rogers and Todd Rogers and family, I love you guys. Emily Silverman for keeping me honest. Rebecca Swanson, Elana Lev Friedland, Cady Vishniac, Micah Neveremer, Dina Dwyer, JD Irpino, Devorah Heitner, Suzanne Clores, Jennifer Lunden: you are all remarkable writers and thinkers and I'm so grateful to know you. Thank you both Kerry

Egan and Alex Marzano-Lesnevich for your support of my work. It means the world to me.

My teachers, mentors, and friends, particularly David Hamilton, Susan Lohafer, Patricia Foster, Bill Lychack, Angie Cruz, Peter Trachtenberg, Jeanne Marie Laskas, Joan Wickersham, Lisa Parker (and David Sogg), Phil Lopate, and Mark Osing.

James Melia, for your patience and enthusiasm. Many thanks also to Lori Kusatzky, Vincent Stanley, Marian Brown, Pat Eisemann, Meryl Levavi, Karen Horton, Christopher Sergio, Hannah Campbell, Kathleen Cook, Kenn Russell, and Janel Brown at Holt. Huge thanks to Eboni Rafus-Brenning.

My parents, Patrick and Cynthia, my in-laws, Nona and Lorne, my brother-in-law Daniel, and my brother Alex, for your love and encouragement.

Holly Katz. What would I do without you? Thank you.

Ori, above everything, for your suppor(t), your banter, your love, the meals you cook, the way you always smell good, for hanging out. How lucky we are. How lucky I am.

Emily Maloney's work has also appeared in *Best American Essays*, *Glamour*, *Virginia Quarterly Review*, the *Washington Post*, and the *American Journal of Nursing*, among others. She has worked as a dog groomer, pastry chef, general contractor, tile setter, and catalog model, and has sold her ceramics at art fairs. Emily has twice been awarded a MacDowell Fellowship. She lives in Evanston, Illinois.